A VERY SHORT,
FAIRLY INTERESTING AND
REASONABLY CHEAP BOOK ABOUT

CROSS-CULTURAL
MANAGEMENT

SECOND EDITION

A VERY SHORT,
FAIRLY INTERESTING AND
REASONABLY CHEAP BOOK ABOUT
INTERNATIONAL
BUSINESS

GEORGE CAIRNS AND
MARTYNA SILWA

A VERY SHORT,
FAIRLY INTERESTING AND
REASONABLY CHEAP BOOK ABOUT
EMPLOYMENT
RELATIONS

TONY DUNDON,
NIALL CULLINANE AND
ADRIAN WILKINSON

FOURTH EDITION

A VERY SHORT,
FAIRLY INTERESTING AND
REASONABLY CHEAP BOOK ABOUT
STUDYING
ORGANIZATIONS

CHRIS GREY

A VERY SHORT,
FAIRLY INTERESTING AND
REASONABLY CHEAP BOOK ABOUT
HUMAN RESOURCE
MANAGEMENT

IRENA GRUGULIS

A VERY SHORT,
FAIRLY INTERESTING AND
REASONABLY CHEAP BOOK ABOUT
KNOWLEDGE MANAGEMENT

JOANNE ROBERTS

Second Edition

A VERY SHORT,
FAIRLY INTERESTING AND
REASONABLY CHEAP BOOK ABOUT
MANAGEMENT

ANN L. CUNLIFFE

A VERY SHORT,
FAIRLY INTERESTING AND
REASONABLY CHEAP BOOK ABOUT
MANAGEMENT RESEARCH

EMMA BELL AND RICHARD THORPE

A VERY SHORT,
FAIRLY INTERESTING AND
REASONABLY CHEAP BOOK ABOUT
QUALITATIVE RESEARCH

SECOND EDITION

DAVID SILVERMAN

A VERY SHORT,
FAIRLY INTERESTING AND
REASONABLY CHEAP BOOK ABOUT
COACHING AND MENTORING

BOB GARVEY

Second Edition

A VERY SHORT,
FAIRLY INTERESTING AND
REASONABLY CHEAP BOOK ABOUT
STUDYING LEADERSHIP

BRAD JACKSON AND KEN PARRY

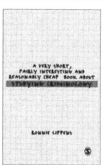

A VERY SHORT,
FAIRLY INTERESTING AND
REASONABLY CHEAP BOOK ABOUT
STUDYING CRIMINOLOGY

RONNIE LIPPENS

A VERY SHORT,
FAIRLY INTERESTING AND
REASONABLY CHEAP BOOK ABOUT
STUDYING STRATEGY

CHRIS CARTER, STEWART R. CLEGG
AND MARTIN KORNBERGER

A VERY SHORT, FAIRLY INTERESTING AND REASONABLY CHEAP BOOK ABOUT

CROSS-CULTURAL MANAGEMENT

JASMIN MAHADEVAN

Los Angeles | London | New Delhi
Singapore | Washington DC | Melbourne

Los Angeles | London | New Delhi
Singapore | Washington DC | Melbourne

SAGE Publications Ltd
1 Oliver's Yard
55 City Road
London EC1Y 1SP

SAGE Publications Inc.
2455 Teller Road
Thousand Oaks, California 91320

SAGE Publications India Pvt Ltd
B 1/I 1 Mohan Cooperative Industrial Area
Mathura Road
New Delhi 110 044

SAGE Publications Asia-Pacific Pte Ltd
3 Church Street
#10-04 Samsung Hub
Singapore 049483

© Jasmin Mahadevan 2017

The title for the 'Very Short, Fairly Interesting and
Reasonably Cheap Book about...Series' was devised
by Chris Grey. His book, *A Very Short, Fairly
Interesting and Reasonably Cheap Book about
Studying Organizations*, was the founding title of this
series.

Chris Grey asserts his right to be recognized as
founding editor of the 'Very Short, Fairly Interesting
and Reasonably Cheap Book about...Series'.

Editor: Matthew Waters
Editorial assistant: Lyndsay Aitken
Production editor: Victoria Nicholas
Copyeditor: Sarah Bury
Marketing manager: Alison Borg
Cover design: Wendy Scott
Typeset by: C&M Digitals (P) Ltd, Chennai, India
Printed by CPI Group (UK) Ltd, Croydon, CR0 4YY

Library of Congress Control Number: 2016954426

British Library Cataloguing in Publication data

A catalogue record for this book is available from
the British Library

ISBN 978-1-47394-823-5
ISBN 978-1-47394-824-2 (pbk)

Dedicated to Io, Fredrik and Peer

Table of Contents

About the author

Jasmin Mahadevan is Professor of International Management with special focus on Cross-Cultural Management at Pforzheim University, Pforzheim, Germany. She received her Master's degree in International Business and Cultural Studies, and her doctoral degree in Cultural Anthropology and Intercultural Communication. Her background can be described as multi-cultural, multi-lingual and multi-ethnic; she has lived an internationally mobile life (with formative experiences in Germany, India, South Africa, the Netherlands, Malaysia, Singapore, the People's Republic of China, England, Wales, the United States, and Japan) and has experienced cross-cultural management as a researcher, as an intercultural trainer and consultant, and as an academic.

Acknowledgements

I wish to thank my family, particularly my parents, and (in alphabetical order) Reinhard Johler, Katharina Kilian-Yasin, Claude-Hélène Mayer, Gabriele Naderer, Henriett Primecz, Markus Pudelko, Laurence Romani and Andreas Steppan. All of them, in one way or another, have contributed to the existence of this book. At Sage, I am very grateful to my editor, Matthew Waters, and his assistant Lyndsay Aitken, and to the five anonymous reviewers commissioned by Sage. I am particularly thankful to Chris Grey for coming up with the fantastic concept of a *Very Short...* book, and to George Cairns and Martyna Śliwa for writing the *Very Short...* book on International Business in this series. Using the latter in class inspired me to write this text. Many thanks go to my academic assistant at Pforzheim University, Iuliana Ancuța Ilie, for her support on this project. Finally, my appreciation goes to all students, colleagues and friends with whom I could exchange my thoughts, and develop and refine the ideas and concepts for this book. Needless to say that all potential interpretative shortcomings of this text are still entirely my own, and that all viewpoints evolve with further learning and over time.

Should you buy this book?

This book is designed for university students, academics and practitioners who wish to learn more about cross-cultural management from multiple angles. Specifically, this book outlines the need and the requirements for a critical cross-cultural management. It is potentially valuable to anyone interested in the subject.

You should buy this book if:

- you want a book about cross-cultural management which you can actually carry around with you while managing across cultures
- you ask yourself questions about 'life, the universe and everything', and feel that you need to have at least some of them answered before it is too late
- you want to develop a personal style of how to manage across cultures, and to better understand yourself and others in the process
- you are bored by obese textbooks
- you don't want to spend too much money.

You should not buy this book if:

- you want to read and follow a manual of 'how to manage across cultures'
- you want bullet points (these are the last ones)
- you just want to pass an exam with minimal effort or function on the job without further thought
- you don't want some of your ideas challenged
- you haven't even got the modest price of this book, or have better things to do with your money

Introduction: towards a critical CCM theory and practice

Cross-cultural management (CCM) is about working (and living) within, across and between cultures; and this book investigates how we might do so in the best possible way and in the best interests of all involved. My intention is to share with you, the reader, a few things about CCM that make sense to me, and this implies that I have favoured some themes over others. The style of this book is conversational, and I have tried to write it as if we were actually having an exchange on CCM (with all the shortcomings that such an approach might have in a printed text).

Specifically, this book sketches the contours of a critical[1] CCM – in the sense of an anthropologically-inspired, power-sensitive and reflexive interplay of multiple CCM theories and methods – and why we might need it. My approach is based on the following considerations. First, I assume that CCM theory and practice should be based on a holistic view of culture, rather than – as seems common in CCM – a selective view, and this is what I mean by an 'anthropologically-inspired', culturally-aware approach. I understand CCM contexts as intertwined with power issues, and this implies that researchers and practitioners should consider the ends to which CCM knowledge is used and by whom. I also propose that those applying CCM tools in practice need to exercise care and develop an understanding as to which tool to use for what purpose and when, and this follows from the interplay of five CCM perspectives which I will outline in the chapters that follow.

In other words, being critical, to me, is a process of re-examining our beliefs, of holding different truths against each other, and of acknowledging a multiplicity of perspectives in their power-laden contexts; it does *not* signify a general state of 'being against' or 'anti-' something. This kind of criticality envisages a 'beyond' and not an 'instead of'; it wishes to add and construct,[2] and it involves you, the reader.

When I speak of 'cross-cultural management' in this book, I refer to the whole of the task of managing within, across, between and beyond cultures – as an international manager, as a 'normal' employee, or simply as a human being living in a culturally diverse society. I assume that 'culture' might refer to *any* collective belonging, for instance, small micro-cultures such as teams, meso-cultures such as organizations, large macro-cultures such as societies and nations, and global and virtual cultures. I also view these collective belongings as being intertwined with power inequalities, and as related to questions of diversity and identity.

Based on this understanding, this book moves beyond established CCM approaches – such as the comparative cross-cultural perspective (Chapter 2) and the intercultural interactionist perspective (Chapter 3) – and includes three additional viewpoints. The cultural perspective (Chapter 1) is based on anthropological thought; it considers culture as a whole and without comparison. The critical multiple cultures perspective (Chapter 4) investigates diversity and multiple identities as equally relevant to CCM as national cultures, and the power-sensitive perspective (Chapter 5) acknowledges the intersections of power, history and knowledge. The cultural perspective, the critical multiple cultures perspective and the power-sensitive perspective are terms of my own; the other two phrases have already been coined.

My approach is based on the assumption that all five perspectives are relevant to a critical CCM theory and practice (despite a mere two of them being standard textbook material). First, we need to investigate the whole of culture, and also as related to our own doings (intra-cultural management), thereby becoming 'culturally aware'. Next, we might compare differences across cultures (cross-cultural management[3]), which enables us to move beyond them via the creation of new (inter-) cultural spheres (intercultural management). We need to do so critically and as related to diversity and multiple identities (critical multiple cultures management), and while paying attention to power effects (power-sensitive management). To my mind, the first three perspectives are the 'basic' sides of the CCM triangle: they concern the classic themes of managing within, across and between cultures. The fourth and fifth are the 'building blocks' of a critical CCM pyramid upon it; they show us a CCM beyond national cultures (e.g. as involving biculturality and hybrid identities) or beyond power inequalities (e.g. as considering the effects of colonialism and imperialism on CCM today). The precondition is that we expose ourselves to situations wherein we can develop and refine our abilities to interplay these perspectives.

A different kind of book?

At its core, this book asks the question of what a critical CCM – in the sense of an anthropologically-inspired, power-sensitive and reflexive interplay of multiple methods – might look like. It also explains why we might need a critical CCM.

In the end, management requires authenticity, and more so if you manage across or in-between cultures. It involves your own cultural backpack as much as the cultural needs of others. As a successful manager in an international, intercultural or global environment, you will need to carefully ask yourself when to adapt, when to be changed by others and when to remain who you are, and you will also need to become aware of the limits of such reflexivity. With regard to your skills and competencies, you will have to find out what to adopt, what to discard and what to keep, and you might need to make this assessment anew in each and every intra-, inter- or cross-cultural situation. This brings about an opportunity for personal growth which goes beyond the managerial sphere: by studying others and trying to walk in their shoes, we might learn more about who we are and who we could be. To me, this is the true excitement of CCM as a critical practice, and the reason why my profession never bores me.

This book is different because: it investigates the 'whole of culture' and not only selected cross-cultural implications of culture; it acknowledges critical diversity and multiple identities as an integral part of CCM; it discusses how power, history and knowledge are intertwined with CCM; it envisages the reflexive interplay of multiple perspectives for moving beyond the paradigms debate in CCM. You will need to find out how this difference matters to you in practice.

CCM as a discipline

CCM has developed out of multiple disciplines. Its specific configuration varies across countries and academic traditions, and the meanings of key terms such as 'cross-' or 'inter-' cultural depend on the theoretical and disciplinary viewpoints they originate from. To understand recommendations for practice, we therefore need to become aware of what is 'meant' if someone speaks of 'cross-cultural management'.

The most prominent CCM subfields are intercultural communication and cross-cultural management.[4] The term *cross*-cultural ('across cultures') implies a cultural comparison ('imagine a Swedish manager needs to manage in Singapore and wishes to understand the relative differences between these cultures'). Conversely, *inter*-cultural ('between cultures') refer to interactions between representatives of different cultures and the possibility of overcoming those differences ('imagine a Swedish manager and a Singaporean manager work together and need to create common understandings'). Still, these differences are not absolute and clear-cut; you could best think of them as different focus points in relation to each other. Matters are complicated by the fact that cross-cultural management is labelled *inter*-cultural management in some academic traditions, for instance in France or Germany, which implies a slightly different, potentially less comparative perspective.

A focus on managerial contexts is implicit with regard to intercultural or cross-cultural *management*, which tends to understand cultural differences in terms of a national or societal culture (e.g. a Swedish managerial style versus a Singaporean managerial style), sometimes with an additional focus on the organizational or corporate level (e.g. a Swedish headquarters versus a Singaporean subsidiary culture). An intercultural *communication* perspective tends to focus more on language and communication as transmitters of culture in intercultural interactions between representatives of different cultures (e.g. the communication between a Swede and a Singaporean). Intercultural communication as a *training and educational* discipline also concerns itself with the development of intercultural competencies (e.g. how can a Swede and a Singaporean communicate successfully?).

With regard to its academic institutionalization, intercultural communication tends to be linked to (foreign) language education. Due to the increasing internationalization of tertiary education worldwide, university-internal language departments are often charged with providing courses on CCM or intercultural communication and competencies to incoming and outgoing students from a variety of disciplinary backgrounds. In non-English-language academic environments, it is often English language teaching staff who are charged with teaching intercultural communication – a view on culture that tends to see language proficiency as the vehicle for intercultural competency, and communication as a key facet of culture.

In academia, intercultural approaches tend to be more prominent in psychology, and language and literary studies, whereas cross-cultural perspectives tend to prevail in management and business. In practice, numerous trainers, coaches and consultants provide a variety of inter- and cross-cultural courses and seminars, and the theoretical foundations of their practice might not always be transparent.

The individual student is seldom introduced to these disciplinary complexities, as programme managers and deans of studies will make a decision for or against a certain disciplinary orientation. Likewise, corporate human resource (HR) managers hiring intercultural trainers in practice might not know upon which disciplinary orientation a specific intercultural training approach is based. Still, a critical CCM starts with being aware of the configurations of the discipline, and this is the reason for why I am sketching its contours.

Issues of power and perspective

Many CCM contexts seem to be linked to issues of power. Take this book, for instance: why have I chosen to write in English? Well, in order to be marketable, this book needs to address a large readership across the globe, and as it happens today, the global *lingua franca* of management and business, as well as many other disciplines, is English, and this development might advantage some over others (Hinds, Neeley and Cramton, 2013; Bjørge and Whittaker, 2015).

Why has the English language become dominant? We can see the influence of certain historical developments (think of European imperialism and colonialism, English naval and military dominance and many other factors) on how 'being international' is defined today (as proficiency in the English language and a certain 'Anglo-American' style of doing things). The mere fact that you are reading this book in English implies that you are either a native speaker or that English is obligatory for, or at least favourable to, your academic or professional success. It also suggests that those who are less fluent in English might be disadvantaged by this expectation and dominant practice.

I am stressing the interlinkages between language and power as an example to make you aware that not everyone has an equal voice in CCM. When a Western European shoe producer and a South Asian production worker meet, it might be only the former one who has the power to define what is meant by 'good' management.

Moving beyond power-discrepancies requires asking prudent questions such as (Flyvbjerg, 2001: 60)[5]: Where are we going? Is this development desirable? What, if anything, should we do about it? Who gains and who loses, and by which mechanisms of power? These questions might be difficult to answer in practice, particularly in the context of CCM, wherein the very concepts of 'good' and 'bad' might not be universal, and not all might be able to influence what is 'right' or 'wrong'.

This book also intends to move beyond the 'paradigms debate' in CCM (Romani, Primecz and Topçu, 2011).[6] A paradigm is an assumption, rule or principle that people within a certain school or discipline accept as true, and the way in which researchers study their object of interest is usually in line within these paradigms (Hatch with Cunliffe, 2006: 1–18).[7] Positivism and interpretivism are two major (CCM) paradigms (Romani, Primecz and Bell, 2014). Positivist scholars believe that the world exists objectively (based on Comte, 1907), whereas interpretative scholars assume that individuals make sense of the world from multiple interpretative viewpoints (Schwartz-Shea and Yanow, 2012: 46). Based on these assumptions, positivist research tends to employ large-scale and quantitative methods for cultural comparison, whereas interpretative studies focus mainly on the in-depth and qualitative analysis of single cultural contexts. Despite these differences, both paradigms view culture as shared by groups of people, and this means that their methods might enrich each other (Romani, Primecz and Topçu, 2011; Mahadevan, 2013).

Based on this understanding, we are required to judge paradigms not categorically, but with regard to their usefulness, and to combine them in the best possible way (Romani, Primecz and Bell, 2014). This book tries to do so. For example, quantitative data from positivist research, e.g. as based on a survey questionnaire, can deliver insights on how large groups of people answer a question such as 'Does family make you feel safe?' If you analyse two large-scale samples, let's say the national cultures of Sweden and Singapore, you can compare the average answers regarding the importance of family to feeling safe. You might then end up with a finding such as 'Family in Sweden is more or less important to feeling safe than in Singapore'.

Providing complementary insights, qualitative data from interpretivist research, e.g. as gathered via narrative-biographical interviews, can deliver in-depth insights on how small groups of people *give meaning* to concepts such as 'family' and 'safety'. For example, 'family' might mean a nuclear family (parents and children) or an extended family (nuclear family plus grandparents, uncles and aunts, cousins, nephews and nieces etc.). In some cultural contexts, it could include in-laws (the family one has married into), in others it might not. There may be different rules regarding 'who marries into whose family' and whether other relations besides the marriage of two individuals of a different sex are the foundational unit of a family or not.

In order to get the whole cultural picture, it might be best to combine both perspectives.[8] You can therefore best think of CCM paradigms as hammers and nails in a carpenter's toolkit: to build a house, you need all these tools combined with the knowledge, skills and experience of when and how to use each tool. As an overall process, your work will require that you combine them. This means that to make a specific decision in a specific situation, you will need to weigh one tool against the other: what do hammers and nails have in common? How are they different? How can I best combine them? Likewise, to best utilize all CCM paradigms, you will need to view them in light of each other and reflexively 'juggle' them in context. This requires you to be aware that no individual CCM paradigm delivers cultural 'truths': rather, they create insights gathered via specific methods as based on specific viewpoints – no more and no less. They are tools to be sharpened by usage, and you are the one to make the decision of which tool to use in which situation.

Such an approach is referred to as *interplay*,[9] and – because we are all a part of the cultures which we wish to investigate – such interplay in CCM needs to be culturally aware and reflexive. Due to the fact that power is intertwined with CCM, this interplay also needs to be power sensitive, and together this is what a critical practice involves. Its requirement is that we expose ourselves to CCM, and when experiencing paradoxical, puzzling or presumably 'strange' situations to try to act as a 'cultural detective' who genuinely cares about solving human puzzles.

A brief outline: what you will find in this book

The main part of this book is composed of five chapters, each covering another CCM perspective. These are relevant to you as a CCM student or practitioner because they result in different viewpoints and tools which you can draw on; their usefulness emerges from your acts of 'juggling' them in practice.

Chapter 1 – the cultural perspective – introduces an anthropologically-inspired approach to CCM, particularly ethnography as a practice-related and empirical method for uncovering culture. This approach is based on the assumption that we should not focus solely on selected aspects of culture when comparing cultures but acknowledge culture as 'that complex whole' (Tylor, 1871: 1) which permeates every aspect of human life. This involves the cultural meanings which we give to the world, the learned and shared cultural knowledge which we cannot put into words, our cultural behaviour and sensory being-in-the-world, and the objects and technology with which we interact. Such awareness of all facets of culture and the skills for interplaying them in context can be considered 'cultural essentials for CCM'.

Chapter 2 – the comparative cross-cultural perspective – introduces tools for comparing relative difference across national cultures. These so-called cultural dimensions are constructed as bipolar opposites ranking cultures on a single scale, for instance, in terms of individualism versus collectivism. They are linked to the question of whether it is justified to simplify cultures this way. To balance this tool, it is suggested that we test cultural hypotheses (such as the assumptions on macro-level cultural difference as put forward by means of cultural dimensions) in specific micro-cultural contexts and from an ethnographic frame of mind. Viewing micro-interpretative and macro-objectivist-level tools in light of each other is another facet of interplay suggested by this book.

Chapter 3 – the intercultural perspective – focuses on intercultural interactions and related concepts such as intercultural competence and cultural intelligence. The intercultural interactionist approach tends to equate culture with communication (in the wider sense); it is based on the assumption that macro-cultural differences will manifest themselves in the micro-cultural interactions between representatives of different cultures. The differentiation between emic (inside) and etic (outside) perspectives is a major tool for facilitating more balanced interactions. Yet, when viewed in light of anthropological ritual theory, it seems that the intercultural interactionist approach is mostly applicable to ritualized interactions (e.g. negotiations) but might not be suitable for complex interactions (e.g. multicultural teamwork). We are therefore required to differentiate between ritualized and complex interactions, and juggle the paradox of cultural regularity and variability. These are further facets of interplay proposed by the book.

Chapter 4 – the critical multiple cultures perspective – investigates multiple identifications: who we are in relation to others and how and why we perceive others as different. It also acknowledges critical diversity markers, such as ethnicity, gender and race, and their power implications. This perspective is not normally part of a CCM book, but it should be as it enlarges our ability to configure CCM in a responsible manner. An investigation into the intercultural training business sheds light on multiple cultures, such as professional and organizational cultures, as well as on the motivations and interests which individuals might have for perceiving others as 'negatively different'. The ability to deconstruct these mechanisms of identification, recognition, marginalization and exclusion is another sphere of interplay required for a critical CCM.

Chapter 5 – the power-sensitive perspective – considers power, history and knowledge in CCM. Whereas the previous chapter investigated power mainly on the micro level of identities in interaction, this chapter assumes that power in all its facets is part of virtually *all* CCM contexts and that we cannot escape its effects; we can only become aware of them. Power is understood as discourse, structure, practice and agency, and as intertwined with knowledge and history, particularly with power-laden developments such as colonialism and imperialism. Its effects are made visible via a discussion of the implicit biases of CCM and intercultural training. The ability to unravel power effects in CCM from specific situations, understood as nodes of power, and as related to all 'frameworks of power' (Clegg, 1989), is another relevant facet of interplay suggested by this book.

Throughout it, I have assumed a critical practice to require an anthropologically-inspired cultural awareness, a grounded powersensitivity and the reflexive interplay of multiple CCM paradigms, perspectives and tools. These themes are also the focus of my concluding remarks.

Notes

1   The so-called *Critical Management Studies*, a discipline which has originated mainly in the United Kingdom but is now internationally relevant, intend to reflect critically upon management and international business. Mats Alvesson and Stanley Deetz (2000) provide an overview.

2   For an overview on critique as a positive and constructive act, please consult Carr (2006).

3   In CCM, the term 'cross-cultural management' refers to the whole discipline, a subfield, *and* to a specific (comparative) perspective within the subfield, as will be made clear in the following. To differentiate between these as clearly as possible, I refer to the discipline as 'CCM', to the subfield as 'cross-cultural management', and to the specific perspective as 'comparative CCM'.

4   Obviously, it is confusing that cross-cultural management is both the umbrella term for a whole discipline *and* a subfield of that discipline. Still, these are the conventions. Please see note 3 on how I use the terms CCM, cross-cultural management, and comparative CCM in this book.

5   The demand of a prudent management and social sciences is based on Aristotle's (2004/1955 [350 BC]) concept of phronēsis, broadly translated as 'practical wisdom' or 'prudence', out of which Bent Flyvbjerg (2001) developed the methodology of a 'phronetic social science'. George Cairns and Martyna Śliwa (2008) have applied phronēsis to international business. To my mind, phronēsis in CCM requires an anthropologically-inspired cultural awareness, reflexivity and power-sensitiveness, which enable us to choose, apply and refine 'good' CCM tools in practice.

6   There are different conceptualizations of paradigms in management and organization studies. The ones most frequently considered in CCM are positivism, interpretivism, postmodernism, critical CCM and postcolonialism (e.g. Deetz, 1992; Alvesson and Deetz, 2000; Jack and Westwood, 2009; Primecz, Romani and Sackmann, 2009; Romani, Primecz and Bell, 2014). Perspectives originating from these five paradigms are discussed in this book.

7   There are several definitions of what a 'paradigm' is. For an overview, please consult Schultz and Hatch (1996), Romani, Primecz and Topçu (2011) and Mahadevan (2013).

8   Mark Saunders, Philip Lewis and Adrian Thornhill (2009: 414–525, 593, 598) provide an overview on positivism and interpretivism, and their respective methods.

9 Interplay is based on the assumption that it is possible to utilize the benefits of multiple paradigms. It is one way of doing so and requires us to look back and forth across paradigms in multiple steps: for instance, first, focusing on the differences; second, focusing on the commonalities; and third, focusing on the connections between paradigms. Other multi-paradigmatic approaches are, for instance, a sequential approach (one after the other) or a simultaneous approach (holding multiple paradigms in mind at the same time). You will find an overview on the debate, including definitions of 'paradigm', in Schultz and Hatch (1996), Romani, Primecz and Topçu, (2011) and Mahadevan (2013).

1

Cultural essentials for CCM

Human beings are influenced by culture while at the same time creating culture through their own doings, and 'good management' itself is a cultural phenomenon. Investigating culture in CCM is therefore tricky (and interesting), as it involves studying the complex cultural world which we take part in. For example, global, multicultural or dispersed teams are an increasingly common feature of the corporate world (Maznevski, 2012). Team members not only bring culture to their work practice but also create new cultures while interacting, and working in this specific team is only one aspect of who they are and what they do.

The phenomenon of global and dispersed teams also reminds us that CCM today is more complex than 'someone being sent abroad' and that it often lacks clear-cut separation lines between the cultures involved. It might therefore be unclear which cultures to consider, where to locate culture and how to overcome perceived difference. This also implies that virtually everyone is somehow involved in CCM. There is no single corporate delegate managing 'the international sphere' and functioning as a 'buffer' for a mainly non-international and local workforce, as might have been the case several decades ago. Rather, we receive international emails, share documents with a colleague in another location, access information from elsewhere and experience global corporate environments (e.g. Gertsen, Søderberg and Zølner, 2012a). To me, this suggests that CCM has become 'normal'; it permeates our social and professional lives, and prior to moving across cultures we will need to consider how culture in general plays a role in our everyday lives.

Still, many CCM texts tend to define culture only randomly (Tipton, 2008: 13–14) or from a biased viewpoint (Fougère and Moulettes, 2011). To overcome this limitation, the chapter highlights how culture is not only part of our CCM practice, but also permeates every aspect of our lives and of how we give meaning to the world. Such a 'cultural perspective' on CCM is linked to interpretivism and qualitative methods (see Introduction); it is informed by social/cultural anthropology and sociology,[1] and to a lesser extent by organization studies. It requires us to become aware of culture as a 'complex whole' (Tylor, 1871: 1) and to split it up into different facets to make it manageable.

As an anthropology-inspired approach to CCM practice, it enables us to overcome the dangers of a culturally-unaware CCM.

Concepts of culture

It is often said that there are hundreds of definitions of culture,[2] and this book is not going to repeat them all. Rather, it proposes five different angles from which to understand the concept holistically and as applied to the requirement of a critical CCM, namely a common-sense approach, culture as 'that complex whole' (Tylor, 1871: 1), culture as shared, learned and social, culture as communities of life versus communities of meaning, and culture as social roles in context.

A common-sense approach

In a common-sense manner, culture refers to a shared understanding of 'how we normally do things around here' (I borrow from definitions of corporate culture, such as 'the way we do things around here'; see Deal and Kennedy, 1982: 60).

Just think about your life and how you 'normally do things'. How do you know how to greet others? How does the greeting differ at university/work, among friends and at home, towards fellow students/colleagues, professors/supervisors and friends, towards members of your family, casual acquaintances and complete strangers? Do others in your immediate surroundings seem to behave in a similar manner? Where does your 'knowledge' of 'how to do these things' originate from? And how many of these 'ways of doing things' are part of you as a manager, engineer, student etc.? Understanding culture as 'how we normally do things around here' reminds us that *any* activity, for instance managing a multicultural and dispersed project-based team, is ultimately a *cultural* activity and cannot be otherwise.

From my experience, culture in management is best identified by asking 'how to see culture?'. We 'see' culture in 'how we normally do things' and cultural differences in 'how others don't normally do things'. For instance, another team member is only perceived as 'culturally different' if we actually experience ('see') something, be it consciously or unconsciously, that is different from what we expect. This makes the common-sense definition of culture as 'the way we normally do things around here' (as opposed to 'how *they* do things around *there*') a good starting point for identifying culture. This insight is also the major reason why this chapter provides seemingly mundane examples. It is in the 'everyday' that culture in CCM begins, and not in the explicitly managerial tasks such as 'leadership', 'managing multicultural teams' or 'conducting negotiations'. Still, the common-sense approach is just the initial step towards culture as an all-encompassing human condition.

Culture as 'that complex whole'

As early as 1871, British anthropologist Edward Burnett Tylor defined culture as

> that complex whole which includes knowledge, belief, arts, morals, law, custom, and any other capabilities and habits acquired by man as a member of society. (1871: 1)

During its time, this definition was ground-breaking in acknowledging that culture is learned and not a biological trait. In particular, Tylor proposed that culture is shared ('man as a member of society'), learned ('acquired') and social (more than one individual is involved; there are always several 'members'), and we will proceed from this assumption. From these features, the overall purpose of culture as generating behaviour and interpreting experience follows. Tylor's (1871) concept of culture necessarily implies cultural diversity (there is more than one 'society'), and the study of differences across cultures was only the next logical step out of which the overlapping disciplines of cross-cultural management and intercultural communication emerged. My previous thoughts on global teams, too, have taken these features for granted. It is only because culture is learned, shared and social *within* but not across groups of people that we encounter cultural differences in global teams and that we might move beyond them via 'un'-learning our initial cultures and 're'-learning a new team culture.

Culture as shared, learned and social

The understanding that the world does not exist objectively but is given 'meaning' by human beings via processes of interpretation is called social constructivism (Berger and Luckmann, 1966). This concept reminds us that none of us views the world objectively, for all of us wear the glasses of our culture(s) when looking at it.

The purpose of culture lies in creating a sense of social predictability: when we encounter others, we do not have to negotiate 'how to normally do things' anew, as culture will provide some answer to what might be expected of us. For instance, when you attend a lecture at university, you do not need to find out anew what 'a lecture' is: assuming that you are not a fresher on your first day at university, you will somewhat 'know' what kind of behaviour is expected of you, based on previous experiences, and you will also be able to identify a 'typical', a 'good' or a 'bad' lecture, based on learned cultural categories. The only way to unlearn this 'way of doing things' would be to go back to being the person you were when attending the first lecture ever – and that is simply impossible. Still, cultural awareness, for instance when asking ourselves how to 'create a team culture', requires just that, namely looking back onto ourselves and trying to understand culture's imprint on us.

Culture also involves a *specific* way of doing things: through exposure to certain groups, individuals learn and are being taught a style of 'how to normally do things', a particular and culture-specific process referred to as enculturation (e.g. M. Mead, 1963). This informs us that culture also limits universal human abilities.

Language is a type of cultural behaviour, and it might help to exemplify this phenomenon. For instance, at birth, human beings possess the universal ability to acquire language capabilities and are also capable of pronouncing every sound any human language might demand. Yet, after having learned a specific mother tongue, this capability is lost, and language-specific sounds such as the English 'th', the German 'ch', the Dutch 'sch', the Spanish 'rr', or the 'kh' in Arabic become difficult or even impossible to pronounce for non-native speakers, depending on the phonetic range which they have learned to pronounce first. This reminds us that whatever we learn, whatever skills, habits or interpretations we acquire, we lose alternative options in the process.

Culture refers to the social dimension of human life, not the biological one. For example, when playing soccer and trying to score, individual soccer players rely on shared cultural knowledge and experiences: they are familiar with the rules of the game and are trained in the same fundamentals of playing soccer. You can therefore identify something like a 'soccer culture'. Likewise, a child of ethnic Han Chinese ancestry who is adopted by Italian parents and grows up in Italy will learn a version of 'Italian culture' – the child will not biologically 'possess' Chinese culture.

This reminds us that we learn culture through others – we do not just 'have' it (no one is 'born' a soccer player) – and that culture always involves more than one individual: we can all be part of many cultures, but none of us 'has a culture'. One of the tricky tasks in global teams is therefore to understand which cultural belonging actually creates relevant differences. Is it a difference in profession, a difference in nationality, a difference in tenure and organizational hierarchy, and so on?

While we are all different somehow, individuals might still share 'something' and orient themselves towards others and what is considered 'normal' by them. After all, 'a way of how to normally do things around here' already implies that a shared 'normality' exists, a so-called 'cultural norm'. For tracing how individuals orient themselves towards others and learn cultural norms, US-American philosopher and social psychologist George Herbert Mead has suggested the concept of the 'generalized other' (his work was posthumously published by Charles Morris in 1934).

For example, upon 'becoming a manager', newcomers to a job will often wonder how to behave based on what they think the other group members expect them to do (wear a business suit, for example). They will also tend to wonder how they might fit into what is considered normal among managers and try to make themselves 'belong' within this cultural norm. Speaking in the terms of G.H. Mead (Mead with Morris, 1934), they relate themselves to the average group member – that is, the generalized other as the representative of invisible, unspoken and often implicit cultural norms. In such a manner, we all develop what I would like to call a 'generalized self': a notion of ourselves as part of a specific group in a specific situation or facet of life. We could therefore assume that a team member who has been part of a global team for longer will have an idea of 'how this team should be normally managed', while a newcomer might not. However, in a project-based and newly-formed team, the presumed 'cultural knowledge' brought about by longer tenure could even be dangerous, as it might result in 'blind spots' towards new and alternative 'ways of doing things' which a newcomer might still be able to envisage.

Social roles in context

Culture also tends to be particular, which means that the guidance which it can provide for understanding 'how things should be normally done' is linked to a specific situation or setting. Simply speaking, culture is connected to 'something', and this 'something' is termed context.[3] For instance, soccer players know how to judge the soccer-playing abilities of others (culture interprets experiences) and what is expected of them while playing soccer (culture generates behaviour), and this is the 'context' wherein they 'share' culture. Conversely, when going to work or university, when being with their respective families, when pursuing other recreational activities, these soccer players might not have much in common (and they also need not have). Likewise, a 'global team culture' might be specific to just the members of this team and only when interacting and for the duration of their working together.

In management and organization studies, as well as in sociology, scholars speak of 'social roles' in order to highlight that, with learning culture, individuals also learn how to represent a certain segment of society, a certain profession, etc. (e.g. Bourdieu, 1977). For example, when 'managing', you make yourself represent this profession in front of your employees, customers and clients. When these distinct social groups meet officially, they tend to behave in line with their respective roles. This means, for example, that top management chairs a strategy meeting and that workers attending ask questions solely during the official 'questions to management' part. However, when meeting elsewhere (for instance, when playing soccer), roles are different in this context, and managers and workers are more equal (unless one of them is a better player, of course, which means that there are other context-specific role requirements and hierarchies to consider). The complexities of culture do not end here: if we move even deeper into specific contexts, we can observe that also the role of being a manager, engineer, worker etc. is differentiated into multiple facets and sub-contexts.

For understanding social roles in, within and across various contexts, Canadian-American sociologist Erving Goffman (1959) has suggested the metaphor of 'social play'. By this, he means that every role has its stage and off-stage. 'Staging' a role takes place frontstage and backstage. For example, when giving a speech at work, managers are 'frontstage': they are expected to play their role convincingly in front of others, their audience. However, when talking in the corridor, managers are 'backstage', which means that they can behave in a more open and flexible manner. They might even chat with workers about how the new corporate strategy is not really what it should be. Still, the managerial role continues to frame the interaction: managers can only critique other managers *because* they themselves *are* managers. This means that also the backstage stages the managerial role (albeit differently); it is only off-stage (for instance, when playing soccer) that the managerial role is not staged at all.

Communities of life and meaning

As Polish-Swedish organizational researcher Barbara Czarniawska (1998: 26) noted (based on Berger and Luckmann, 1995), culture involves communities of life and communities of meaning. Communities of life, such as a local group or a family, can be pinpointed to a specific location; their cultural patterns often have a beginning and an end. To investigate communities of life, we can understand their contexts in terms of space and time, and as a local phenomenon (see also Strathern et al., 1987).

Conversely, communities of meaning, which are particularly relevant to CCM, emerge beyond a specific location and point in time. Think, for example, of spheres such as 'Apple world' (Garsten, 1994) or 'Wall Street' (Ho, 2009). The first refers not only to a transnational company with multiple locations and its relations, but also to its products and the image and lifestyle associated with them. Wall Street is not only a specific location in Manhattan, but also a financial nexus with numerous interconnections and worldwide implications. Most of us move through different cultural spheres and are part of multiple communities of meaning throughout the course of a single day. Therefore, when studying communities of meaning, we should assume that the cultural context wherein culture needs to be investigated cannot be fixed to a specific locality. Rather, context refers to the ways in which interpretation is connected to 'something' (Dilley, 1999), whether this is a specific group of people, a virtual space, certain objects, a conflict between two parties, etc.

For instance, a multinational corporation such as McDonalds, Nestlé, Philips or Samsung is not only a corporate entity, but also a cultural sphere encompassing multiple communities of meaning. Meaning in multinational companies also tends to be linked to the aim to transmit 'culture' and 'corporate values' from headquarters to subsidiary (Gertsen, Søderberg and Zølner, 2012b). This reminds us that managerial meaning-making and meaning-giving not only take place across multiple contexts but are also linked to corporate hierarchies and issues of power. Understanding companies this way can deliver helpful insights into team cultures, organizational cultures, professional cultures, etc. and how they shape individual perceptions and behaviour within certain 'frameworks of power' (a term coined by Clegg, 1989).

Cross-cultural implications of culture

Culture not only creates similarities among groups of people, it also makes them different from other groups of people, and it's impossible to have one cultural phenomenon – similarity or difference – without the other. Cultural differences, too, are not 'given' but learned. For instance, toddlers do not yet differentiate between categories of human beings – it is the adults who have learned to perceive 'the English', 'the German', 'the French' (I am using random examples here) as different, and they indeed have been made different from each other via enculturation. This reminds us that cultural differences lie in the eye of the beholder, and the beholder is a cultural being as well. So, we can only investigate how difference is 'perceived' in a specific CCM context and make assumptions as to the origins of these perceptions – we cannot tell whether this difference is 'real', even though it 'feels' real to those involved.

How much difference is too much difference? Erving Goffman (1974) suggests that individuals refer to so-called frames of reference for organizing their experience. Frames are assumed to structure an individual's, a group's or a society's perception of the social world and to guide them in their behaviour. We could therefore say that 'too much' of difference in interpreting cultural meaning arises if we and others who experience the same context cannot link ourselves to shared frames of reference. For example, if we have learned that 'ice-breaking' jokes are part of on-stage managerial performance, we might find a facts-based presentation dull and uninspiring leadership. On the other hand, if our team members, originating from another culture, have learned that good leaders should be sober, non-emotional and facts-oriented, they might consider a joking management to be overly frivolous and not to be trusted. To check where you stand on this matter, you might search the internet for Steven Ballmer's (2001) performance in front of Microsoft employees. You will see him jumping up and down on the stage, exhausting himself with exclamations of 'I love this company'. Just ask yourself – is this a convincing leadership performance, and why or why not?

To create our respective realities, culture provides us with categories with which to structure the world. The question is whether we are able to unlearn categories such as 'good leadership and how to see it', and what these categories do to us and others in the role of cross-cultural managers. We can also expect these categories to originate from life experiences beyond the managerial sphere. There are, for instance, more words for a 'not so clear sky' in the English language (fog, mist, haze, etc.) than in German (just 'Nebel'). If different types of 'Nebel' do not exist in German, can we think of them? We might therefore wonder whether we can conceive of 'leadership concepts' for which our respective mother tongues do not have words.

Or, on an even more profound level, a language such as Mandarin Chinese determines meaning largely via word order whereas word stems remain unchanged and uncategorized. Indo-European languages distinguish between nouns, verbs and adjectives and change these words via different tenses, declinations and conjugations. Bahasa Indonesia (Indonesian) 'glues' and combines a seemingly endless variety of prefixes, suffixes or infixes to a word stem, and this is the main means of establishing categorizations and meaning. This implies that Mandarin Chinese and Indonesian provide options unknown to Indo-European languages. Conversely, other concepts, such as tenses, exist in neither Mandarin Chinese nor Indonesian. We might therefore wonder if the ways in which individuals 'understand' the world are *really* the same across all these languages (for example, what is the concept of time if there are no explicit tenses but, let's say, flexible markers of anteriority and posteriority?). If we transfer this linguistic insight to the general level of culture, we need to ask: can it *really* be that individuals across these cultures process the same CCM theories similarly, share ideals of good leadership, and have comparable ways for how to conceive the world and themselves within it?

We should therefore seriously doubt that our 'way of normally doing things' is more than just one of many ways of doing things. This implies that no cultural categories are 'right' or 'wrong', for the world is neither characterized by concepts such as 'tenses' or 'prefixes', nor by the categories 'fog' and '*Nebel*'. Likewise, each management style is just a limited, culture-based and arbitrary connection of 'how things work', 'what things mean' and 'how things should be done' – it is not an objective managerial reality, even though it might seem otherwise (at a certain point in your life, you just seem to 'know' how to manage). Unfortunately, and as a cultural drawback, this learned repertoire is only helpful within familiar managerial contexts and among similar individuals; it might actually lead to wrong clues in other contexts and with members of other cultures. *Cross*-cultural management implies being aware that we do *not* know how to manage and that we should never become too sure of our ways of doing things.

Based on this awareness, we can conclude that, in a multicultural and dispersed project-based team, individual team-members will bring 'different ways of how we have learned to normally do things' to this context. Ideally, these differences will then be replaced by a new and shared 'common way of doing things' that is in the best interest of all team members. As cross-cultural managers, we are required to support this process of cultural integration, move beyond our respective cultural blind spots, and facilitate mutual learning.

Facets of culture

As the previous considerations imply, it might be impossible to grasp culture 'as a whole' for the purposes of CCM and its complex contexts, such as multicultural and dispersed teams. To my mind, the question to be asked is not 'what is culture?' but rather 'how to split it up?' in order to make it small and manageable.

Obviously, a lot has happened since 1871 ('the world has changed', as one of my favourite movies proclaims in its opening scene). Nevertheless, key elements of Tylor's definition still hold true: culture remains shared, learned and social; it makes groups of people more similar to each other and more different from other groups of people; it has visible and invisible elements (e.g. behaviour versus knowledge), and material and immaterial facets (e.g. arts versus beliefs). All these facets of culture are part of management today, and therefore need to be recognized as cultural essentials for CCM.

At the same time, these elements might need some 'updating'. For example, how to locate the borders between cultures in a fast-paced and globalized world (Tylor speaks of 'societies')? What about technology as a new cultural facet (as still 'material culture')? To tackle these questions, the following pages propose specific features of culture, namely cultural knowledge, cultural meaning, cultural behaviour, cultural being-in-the-world, and objects and technology (material culture). These depart from culture as 'a complex whole' but also move beyond it. Their purpose is to make culture in CCM small and manageable.

Cultural knowledge

How do we know what we know? Imagine you meet another person in the multinational company where you work whom you have never encountered before, and you are asked to work together on a specific project. You chat for a while and realize that you have virtually nothing in common. The other person seems 'very different'. How do you overcome this difference? The problem is that you are not sure what creates this feeling of initial difference. Is it another profession or nationality, a different age group or upbringing, an alien departmental culture, and so on? Where do you even begin to understand the other person and their cultural identifications? How do you create something like 'team spirit'? Might it not be sensible to ask, 'could you please tell me which groups you identify with and why you do the things the way you do them?'

Unfortunately, theory suggests that you won't get an explicit answer to such questions, as quite often culture cannot be put into words; it is, in the words of Hungarian-British chemist and social scientist Michael Polanyi (1967), largely 'tacit'. Tacit knowledge is nothing like knowledge from a textbook (prescriptive, clearly defined, etc.). Instead it refers to an immediate and often fuzzy sense or feeling of 'this is how it is/should be' which – in contrast to explicit knowledge – cannot be put into words. Simply speaking, we know more than we can tell (Polanyi, 1967: 4),[4] and cognitive anthropology (D'Andrade, 1995) focuses on such cultural knowledge and related thinking patterns which seem self-evident but can hardly be explained.

Cultural knowledge – as opposed to personal knowledge – refers to the social dimension of human beings (generalized self and other). It involves the *learned* and *shared* understanding of 'how things are normally done'. This suggests that culture as 'that complex whole' is largely tacit. For example, we can note that the appropriate speaking distance between individuals is culturally learned (there is no universal distance which everyone on the globe observes), and this can be considered an element of tacit culture (E.T. Hall, 1959). In a multicultural team, this might create discomfort. You may feel that the other person is putting pressure on you concerning the team outcome – but actually they are just standing 'too close'. Or you might feel that another person is disinterested in your part of the project – but actually they are just 'too far away'. This reminds us that being a manager, a PR executive, an engineer, etc. encompasses more than words can say – it is just 'known' and 'done' collectively; tacit knowledge potentially ingrained in the generalized self. Based on this insight, observing and experiencing culture will tend to deliver more insights than asking questions about culture. Therefore, managing across cultures is also an exercise in observation and learning from experience as well as being reflexive with regard to our own tacit assumptions and related behaviour.

Cultural meaning

Some CCM scholars (e.g. Romani, Sackmann and Primecz, 2011) have proposed focusing on cultural meaning instead of cultural knowledge. This approach can be linked to interpretative and symbolic cultural anthropology as put forward by US-American anthropologist Clifford Geertz (1973). The idea behind this is that 'knowledge', even 'tacit knowledge', is too rational a concept to approximate how culture interprets experience and generates behaviour. The key question to a meaning-related perspective on culture is not 'how do we know what we know?', but rather 'what do things *mean* and how is this meaning produced?' For example, just think of concepts such as 'fairness', 'good leadership', 'a pleasant work environment'. How come we are able to recognize fairness in our colleagues, be motivated by good leadership and choose a pleasant work environment for ourselves? Or, conversely, why do we feel that someone whom we perceive as culturally different is 'not fair', a 'bad manager', or an 'annoying co-worker'? For example, the degree to which managers are expected to express compassion for others varies considerably across different societies (Chhokar, Brodbeck and House, 2007), suggesting that, in some social environments, a caring and emotional manager is likely to be perceived as a 'good leader' whereas in others the same behaviour might be interpreted as overly emotional and thus incompetent. Or, at a more simple level, does it seem okay to you if your – male – manager starts crying in the office about a bad project outcome or does this prove that he has lost it?

In abstract terms, culture provides shared and learned clues as to how a certain situation (what is happening?) should be interpreted (what does it mean?). A cultural outsider can only observe visible behaviour, yet might fail to grasp the underlying meaning, as they may link visible signs (actions, words, objects, etc.) to underlying meaning in a different manner. A presumably simple sign, such as a smile, might be intended to express joy, rejection, anger, frustration, affection and many more emotions (and all of these expressions have been identified in some culture or another).

A CCM worst-case scenario emerges if you confuse a colleague's smile of frustration with a smile of joy or your project partner's smile of rejection with a smile of agreement. Such discrepancy suggests that the links between visible behaviour or aspects of culture and their underlying cultural meaning are socially constructed, potentially specific to only a certain group of people and not self-evident. It also points to the fact that there is more to the cultural norm than you might think of at first sight. For example, why and how is showing emotions (not) okay in the office? Could you *really* explain this to others?

We can say that culture expresses invisible meaning and enables us to recognize this meaning in others. Culture does so by providing a link between (invisible) meaning and (visible) cultural elements, and the glue holding them together is symbolic. Symbols *mean* more than they are, in academic terms: they have not only an immediate (denotative) but also a wider (connotative) meaning (Van Maanen, Manning and Miller, 1996). For example, a flag represents more than just a piece of cloth. A smile is not only a facial expression it also conveys values. Crying in the office is not only the expression of an emotion it also says something cultural about 'good leadership'.

Symbolic meaning can be conveyed via multiple forms, such as words, behaviour, contexts or objects (Jones, 1996: 5–6). At the level of language, symbolic meaning is often expressed via the use of culture-specific terms (characteristics of 'the way we normally talk around here'), so-called folk terms (McCurdy, Spradley and Shandy, 2005: 36–37). For instance, there are freshers at every university. However, at the specific university where I was a fresher, this group was and still is referred to as 'squeakies' (actually, 'Quietschies' in the German original), and this term conveys a context-specific symbolic meaning. The story that unfolds from it is that some buildings at this university were centuries old, and whenever a door was opened, it inevitably squeaked. Freshers everywhere seem to get locations mixed up, and at this university they were noticed for making the wrong doors 'squeak'. Similarly, the language used in companies delivers insights into cultural meanings and how they differ across sites, departments, teams, and so on.

Likewise, employees might tell each other stories which carry a symbolic meaning (Boje, 2008), a cultural phenomenon referred to as 'folklore' (Jones, 1996: 9). Many companies also have an 'organizational saga' (Clark, 1972), that is a shared, learned and social story of how the company was founded or why it prospered. I once encountered a tale of how three middle managers crossed the Baltic Sea in a sailing boat one weekend to convince a potential investor in his Swedish summer house to finance their company when it was on the brink of bankruptcy, and as the organizational saga goes this heroic action was supposed to have saved the day.

Cultural symbols tend to allow for multiple interpretations (Jones, 1996). This means that the symbolic meaning attached to an object, person, action and so on, is not an fixed and singular definition: even members of the same cultural group might interpret shared symbols differently, these meanings might differ and change across contexts and time, and that is the internal heterogeneity of culture (the sailing boat tale was told differently by different people, but still, key elements, such as who are the heroes and the villains of the story, were retained).

Ultimately, culture is both: sufficiently homogeneous enough to feel 'at home' within a group, to share 'ways of normally doing things', tacit knowledge, symbols and interpretations and so on, but also heterogeneous enough to allow for internal diversity and cultural change. For example, after a political crisis, the flag might change its meaning in the eyes of a part of a country's population, and, ultimately, the cultural norm might change as well. Or, the sailing boat tale might be reinterpreted as an act of desperate management which should never be repeated (this might happen in times of organizational change which demands for new sensemaking). Still, even with change, you will find *patterns* of symbolic meaning which are more than arbitrary, and this is the shared and learned cultural dimension of how we understand the world.

Cultural behaviour (habitus)

According to French sociologist Pierre Bourdieu (1977), human beings also tend to reproduce pre-reflexive and non-cognitive elements of culture via their behaviour and their 'way of being', a concept called habitus.

Habitus unites groups of people and distinguishes them from other groups of people. For example, when observing students at your home university, you might be able to guess their majors: as a rule, engineering students dress and behave differently from management students, from design students, and so on. Obviously, your guess will not always be right, but most of the time it may well be. Likewise, in a company you might be able to guess who is a manager and who is a worker, who is a technician and who is part of the canteen crew, simply by observing their 'way of being', their habitus. At the same time, you are likely to display a certain habitus as well, which makes you similar to some and distinguishes you from others. Paying attention to these everyday facets of culture, for instance, by observing dress codes or routines in the corporate canteen of a multinational company, will tell you something about CCM.

Habitus is linked to cultural behaviour, yet it goes deeper as it includes a 'way of being' which precedes actual behaviour. At work, habitus becomes relevant with regard to so-called communities of practice (based on Bourdieu, 1977; see also Orr, 1996). Communities of practice are united by symbolic practice. This means that in order to show that they possess the required know-how and expertise, members of the community of practice need to express a certain habitus. For example, nutrition specialists need to 'look' fit and healthy; personal trainers cannot be obese; undertakers need to be dressed and groomed conservatively; medical doctors need to evoke trustworthiness, and so on.

Shared habitus even exists if a certain professional practice is invisible to others; it is then channelled into another, 'everyday', behaviour (Orr, 1996). For example, software developers need to possess stamina and endurance when developing code in order to achieve technological excellence. In order to trust each other, they need to rely on each other's capabilities, and usually, it is individual practice that assures other members of the community of these capabilities. However, an individual software developer works in sole interaction with their computer – others, even members of the same community of practice, do not see this practice. Therefore, they cannot be sure that a fellow software developer actually possesses the stamina and endurance required for technological excellence. This implies that the community of practice needs to find other symbolic ways of expressing this ideal. These symbolic ways can be seemingly mundane. For example, in the context of research and development engineering, I have often observed long-distance running during lunch hours or bike racing to and from work, be it in Silicon Valley or in similar European or East Asian clusters. From a community-of-practice perspective, this might signify a physical way of expressing the 'virtual stamina' required for technological excellence.

In summary, a community-of-practice approach to CCM pays attention to the ways in which a certain habitus is expressed at work and acknowledges its relevance to multicultural team work. This means that should you observe long-distance running or bike racing among your research engineers, a simple thing such as investing in showers and a locker room might be key to bringing together engineers from different national cultures and creating a common 'team spirit'.

Cultural being-in-the-world (embodiment and dress)

Going even further than habitus, phenomenology assumes that sensory experiences precede knowledge, interpretation and meaning-making (based on Merleau-Ponty, 1965). For example, you can only 'know' a stone after having stumbled across it; it is only then that you give it the meaning of an obstacle to be overcome. Likewise, you need to experience bike racing; you cannot 'know' it.

Phenomenology is an often neglected, but relevant part of corporate life. I have heard software developers speak of code as 'their baby', and I have seen workers caress a machine and observed managers 'smell' the atmosphere of a meeting. Across cultures, it is often sensory experiences that create an overwhelming sense of difference or belonging. For example, I have books from my father's student years in India which still have a specific 'Indian mothballs smell' that seems to linger on wherever I keep them, and reminds me of my own childhood in India. Likewise, I just *know* how Dutch *bitterballen* (a really interesting deep-fried partly meat dish) are supposed to taste, and experiencing that taste every once in a while will inevitably surface powerful memories of my student years in the Netherlands of which I had not been aware for years. This reminds us that we need to acknowledge such sensations and consider them a relevant source of managerial knowledge and cross-cultural conflict.

A major aspect of our 'being-in-the-world' is embodiment. It assumes that we experience the world through the body, and that the body is the means by which we express culture (Csordas, 1990). Embodiment becomes relevant when invisible concepts such as 'competency', 'leadership', 'trust', etc. are involved. For instance, many professions are based on the implicit assumption of ableism, and the 'disabled body' tends to be undervalued (Mik-Meyer, 2016). So what happens in the above mentioned scenario if a software developer is not able-bodied, cannot bike race to and from work, and is therefore doubted in her or his professional abilities?

Bodies at work in general tend to be classified, rated and judged (Tretheway, 1999). British organizational researcher Fiona Moore (2015a: 224), for instance, reports that when speaking about 'working on a final assembly line in an automobile plant' to academic colleagues and those working in the automobile industry, she encountered 'surprise that "a little woman" would be capable of doing such a job'. To this statement, Moore herself adds: 'I am 163 centimetres tall, average height for a woman in the UK, and muscular.' So, how does this body become 'too little', and the job itself 'unsuitable for women'? (That is the perception of the male majority at BMW MINI in Cowley, the cross-cultural organizational context studied by Moore, 2015a.)

Linked to embodiment are the objects we decorate our bodies with in order to present ourselves to the world – that is, our clothing and dress. These convey important symbolic meaning (Durham, 1999) and are used to show who we are (or who we are not) (Rafaeli and Pratt, 1993). Dress contributes to habitus (Durham, 1999: 390–391), and from this perspective, the wrong choice of dress might be just as disastrous to your management career as making a wrong strategic decision.

Embodiment and dress are linked to habitus (see the previous sub-section), and all three are intertwined with power effects (Clegg, 1989: 153–158). For example, the knowledge of 'how to carry and dress the managerial body' comes easier to those who have this symbolic under-standing already ingrained in their bodies and senses (because they have been born into the 'managerial social class' and not into the 'working class').

Together, habitus, embodiment and dress inform us that human beings possess not only economic capital, but also the cultural and social capital for succeeding at work (Bourdieu, 1983, 1986). Together, they form the symbolic capital which enables individuals to achieve status, exercise power and be recognized. For example, the right academic degree only pays off in terms of money and career (economic capital) if it's supplemented with the culturally 'right' habitus (as based, for instance, on social class), the right way to dress and the right way of showing or not showing competency (social and cultural capital). Obviously, this socio-culturally 'right' way is not the only way for how things might be done, but it is the way in which those already occupying aspired-to positions define 'how to do things'. The situation might be aggravated if the individual body is not even the presumably right kind of (slim, fit, able) body expected in context, and this suggests that – even though culture does not refer to the biological dimension of human beings – cultural *meanings* are attached to our biology, the implications of which need to be considered by CCM (see Chapter 4).

Objects and technology (material culture)

Not all cultural spheres are limited to human beings and their thoughts, behaviour and sensory experiences. Some involve material culture, namely objects and technology (Latour, 1996; Hicks and Beaudry, 2010), and we all have learned cultural ways of handling them (e.g. Honold, 2000). For instance, how does a group of students know where to sit in a lecture room? Why do they sit on chairs and not on tables? Why does no one sit down on the lone chair facing the rest of the class (unless they want to disturb the social order)? It seems that students have learned the culture-specific symbolic meaning of objects and space: they are aware of their culture-specific purposes and usage, and even a student violating those unspoken norms would be aware that they are doing so.

At work, such 'knowledge of objects' often involves specialized knowledge. For example, 'knowing how to operate a certain machine' is key knowledge among certain technicians, and they might even have a gut feeling with regard to some machines or like or dislike some piece of equipment more than another (Orr, 1996).

Many professions have developed their own symbolic patterns of how to represent objects and technology, and their meanings. For instance, when trying to exchange arguments for or against a specific design, engineers and architects often do not rely on words, but tend to visualize their ideas via technical drawings – a shared professional language which is based on the symbolic representation of objects. In some corporate environments humans actually work hand in hand with complex hard- and software combinations, such as production robots, and use symbolic representations, e.g. steering software, to understand these non-human counterparts. On a more simple technological level, we learn culture-specific ways of 'what good slides should look like', 'how I should name my files' and 'how my team members should file a change report'.

Technical work contexts become increasingly 'cross-cultural', and many CCM contexts, such as multicultural and dispersed teams, have become unthinkable without objects, such as smartphones, laptops and other equipment, and technology, such as the world wide web, shared server spaces and 'clouds'. Together, both developments introduce humans to a material cultural sphere that is comprised of physical objects and intangible technology. For instance, we may become angry at a corporate intranet when failing to download files, and we may actually care about the production robots with whom we work. This reminds us that non-humans (such as online platforms or complex machines) are not only products of material culture to be used by us, but also independent cultural actors with whom we as humans interact (Latour, 1996).

Towards an anthropology-inspired CCM practice

Based on the previous considerations, we can summarize that culture is socially learned and shared and creates perceived similarities and difference. Culture also establishes a sense of social predictability: when encountering the unknown, we tend to structure a situation in terms of what we already know, interpret new experiences through cultural knowledge we've already acquired, and base our future behaviour on behaviour that seems to have proven successful in the past. The interrelations between culture and ourselves are paradoxical: we learn culture through others, thereby perpetuating it. Yet, we also change culture through our doings and create new 'cultures' in the process. This makes us both products and producers of culture, a process which involves knowledge, meaning, behaviour, being-in-the-world, and objects and technology. Culture is also largely tacit and experienced beyond words and rational thought.

So, how to become aware of 'that complex whole' (Tylor, 1871: 1) and ourselves as part of it? Or, to borrow a metaphor from cross-cultural researchers Fons Trompenaars and Charles Hampden-Turner (1997), how can fish become aware of water?

To my mind, CCM begins with the insight that there is 'water' all around us: we all employ cultural perspectives on the world, all of which are limited, and none of which represent the 'real world'. As a complex whole, culture provides us with plausible answers to what things might 'mean', and these answers tend to be shared only among a certain group of people or within a certain context. Based on this insight, a culturally-aware common-sense definition of culture might best describe it as 'the way in which we have *come* to normally do things around here *and in this specific context*'. Linked to this insight is the understanding that '*what people do must seem plausible or feel right to them – otherwise, they wouldn't do it*'. We should also remember that behaviour, interpretation and how the two are linked might differ across cultures.

Culture is a complex whole and understanding CCM solely in terms of selected cultural facets, such as communication (see Chapter 3), knowledge (e.g. Holden, 2002) or business behaviour (e.g. Gesteland, 2012), might lose sight of 'that complex whole', particularly our sensory being-in-the-world, and objects and technology as non-human CCM actors. Based on the cultural perspective, we should acknowledge that CCM cannot be 'known' or fully put into words, but rather needs to be done, perceived, experienced and felt. This involves trying to find plausible answers to 'how we perceive the world' which we might then make explicit to others. It requires us to bring those cultural meanings and elements of tacit culture 'to the surface' which are hidden to others and, potentially, to ourselves.

The dangers of culturally-unaware CCM

Conversely, culturally-unaware CCM is associated with the dangers of ethnocentrism, naïve realism and native categories, and othering. Ethnocentrism, a term coined by US-American sociologist William Sumner in 1906, refers to 'a view of things that one's own group is the centre for everything, and all others are scaled and rated with reference to it' (Sumner, 1906: 13). Ethnocentrism tends to undervalue alternative worldviews and presume that our own cultural orientation or managerial style is superior. In a multinational company, this might lead to local managers adapting to headquarters' conventions, preventing the company from utilizing the strengths of all potential managerial styles available and leading to its losing sight of local markets (Perlmutter and Heenan, 1974).

Linked to ethnocentrism is naïve realism, the 'taken-for-granted belief that the way in which we perceive the world is how the world actually is' (McCurdy, Spradley and Shandy, 2005: 9). Naïve realism might result in native categories, that is, taken-for-granted cultural assumptions (see Moore, 2015a, 2015b; based on Buckley and Chapman, 1997), such as thinking that working on an automotive assembly line is 'nothing for women' (Moore, 2015a).

Those subjected to native categories are often 'othered'. Othering describes a process of making others more alien than they actually are, mainly in order to affirm people's own identity and power positions (Jackson II and Hogg, 2010: 520). In Moore's (2015a) example, it is the male majority of managers and workers in the automotive industry who affirm their identity and their power position on the job by constructing the category 'female' as the inferior outsider. However, it might also be a whole country's business culture which is portrayed as overly exotic and traditional (Moore, 2015b). The critical consequences of such processes are considered in Chapters 4 and 5 of this book.

Based on the understanding that culture is done, felt and perceived, culturally-unaware CCM might also originate from the implicit assumption that culture is cognitive and rooted in communication. Most of the previous examples have nothing to do with cognition and rational choice, but nonetheless weigh heavily on managerial style and leadership expectations. They show that culture is largely tacit, experienced and felt.

Participant observation as a CCM tool

For acknowledging and investigating culture as 'that complex whole' in practice, anthropology has suggested the method of participant observation, also referred to as fieldwork or ethnography (e.g. Spradley, 1980).[5] Its strength lies in the ability to investigate culture beyond explicit knowledge, thought and words. In short, participant observation can uncover tacit culture.

Participant observation was first put forward by social anthropologist Bronislaw Malinowski (1922), partly out of sheer necessity and specific circumstances. Malinowski first earned a doctoral degree in mathematics and physics in his home town Krakow (then part of the Austro-Hungarian Empire). Later, he studied in Leipzig and at the London School of Economics, focusing on the Aboriginal people of Australia. In 1914, Malinowski was accompanying an anthropologist to the island of New Guinea, the southern part of which was annexed by Australia as part of the British Commonwealth. At that point, World War I broke out and as an Austrian subject and enemy of the British Commonwealth, Malinowski should have been detained. However, he managed to obtain permission from the Australian government to undertake ethnographic research in their territories. He ended up staying on the Trobriand Islands in Melanesia for two years, and it was from this experience that he developed the method of participant observation.

Participant observation requires a researcher's longitudinal immersion into the culture of those studied (for an overview see Spradley, 1980). In contrast to detached observation, where the researcher is present but not involved, participant observation demands (inter-)action. The researcher should, for example, learn the language of those studied, engage in their day-to-day activities and participate in social events.[6]

Based on its original focus, fieldwork should last at least a year, following the assumption that the anthropologist needs to experience a full year's cycle (from harvest to harvest) in order to learn the culture of a traditional community (obviously, this rule is not that strict for the modern corporation, but it gives you an estimate of how laborious the method is and what 'longitudinal' means from an anthropological perspective). In its present form (I am simplifying), ethnography implies that we should not predefine what culture encompasses but instead learn culture in its context. This requires us to acknowledge culture as 'that complex whole' and to juggle its different facets in order to find out which one is relevant in the context and how. From there, we can gain new insights into reality and the patterns of culture in context.

For instance, Fiona Moore's (2015a) anthropological investigation at BMW/Mini shows that embodiment is a relevant cultural facet in context: it enables us to understand the roots and consequences of the dominant perception that 'production work is nothing for women'. This insight could only be gained by the researcher experiencing culture herself and via her (female) body, towards whom the male majority reacted in culturally-relevant ways. We can now see that the abilities of female production workers, and maybe of female employees in general, are undervalued. This allows us to consider options for moving beyond this 'taken-for-granted belief'.

So, should we all take a year off to go study culture? Certainly not, but perhaps we could approach our daily lives a bit more anthropologically. This means that wherever you are, and whatever you do, you can investigate the experience in a way that is 'anthropologically inspired' (Czarniawska, 1998: 19). You are doing your job (in CCM) anyway, so you may as well think of yourself as an 'amateur ethnographer', who is participating in CCM while at the same time trying to observe themself and others, and to make sense of this experience and infer cultural patterns.

Notes

1   Anthropology, the discipline that studies culture, is the major source for concepts of culture. The purpose of this chapter is not to re-tell anthropological history, rather to ask those cultural questions which are relevant to bringing about cultural awareness for CCM. Any text about anthropological concepts of culture, their different traditions (for instance, the differentiation into social and cultural anthropology, or into structural functionalism and symbolic interpretivism) and their further development in related disciplines, such as sociology, would be a book of its own (or several, as it were: Eriksen, 2010, and Eriksen and Nielsen, 2013, provide overviews). Furthermore, the study of culture has seen several 'turns', each of them enriching the understanding of culture in various disciplines. Of course, and like in every discipline, this development was not value-free: some concepts of culture became 'in vogue', others were regarded as old-fashioned, and different waves of what was considered 'cutting edge' washed over those studying culture (Barnard, 2000; Bachmann-Medick, 2009).

2   At this point, the 164 definitions of American anthropologists Alfred Kroeber and Clyde Kluckhohn (1952) tend to be routinely cited.

3   Context might be one of the anthropological concepts that are the most difficult to understand. It refers to the frameworks of a situation, interaction or experience without involving fixed categories of what constitutes 'context'. Originally, based on the anthropological focus on small microcultures, context is a specific point in time or a specific location, e.g. a tribe, a community, an organization. However, more recently, as anthropologists

have come to study so-called cultural flows, e.g. 'Wall Street' (Ho, 2009) or capitalism as a concept, 'context' has come to mean a sphere, a phenomenon, the blurry border of where 'meaning' ends. For details, see Strathern et al. (1987), Dilley (1999) and Marcus (1995).

4   Some scholars have put forward the idea that tacit knowledge is a hidden resource, for example among knowledge workers, to be mobilized via proper management (Nonaka and Takeuchi, 1995), for instance, in the area of CCM (Holden, 2002). However, the conversion of tacit to explicit knowledge might simply be impossible, for we can never be sure from where our sense of 'knowing things' originates (based on Polanyi, 1967: 195; e.g. Tsoukas, 2003). For more details, you might consult Carter, Clegg and Kornberger (2008), in this series.

5   Actually, in anthropology, ethnography tends to refer more to an overall research perspective and to the outcome of anthropological research, namely its written account. The actual process of research is usually referred to as fieldwork; participant observation is the prime method while doing fieldwork. However, in management and organization studies, ethnography has come to mean the research method itself. I am following this convention in this book.

6   Traditionally, anthropologists like Malinowski set out to study small communities, called a 'field', mostly outside their own society. By now, ethnography has also been applied to other contexts, for example, organizations or culture 'at home', and to CCM.

2

Comparative CCM

The previous chapter looked at culture from within and suggested that it provides individuals with a shared, learned and social sense of 'this is how things work' and 'this is how the world is'. To manage this condition, we first need to make culture 'large' and acknowledge it as 'that complex whole', which involves not only knowledge, meaning and behaviour, but also our sensory 'being-in-the-world', and objects and technology. In a second step, we need to make culture 'small' again by interplaying its different facets in context.

This chapter takes a view *across* cultures; it introduces the comparative CCM perspective and its major tool, so-called cultural dimensions (sometimes also referred to as cultural orientations or cultural value orientations) by which national or societal cultures can be compared. This tool enables us to uncover a relative (but not absolute) difference between macro-level cultures.

The differentiation between relative and absolute cultural difference is important to bear in mind. Let's say you are travelling to a foreign country xyz for the first time. You wish to prepare yourself for how the citizens of this country are most likely to behave. You might find guidance online and in various books, although this information will only be helpful if you compare it to what you are used to. Imagine the business etiquette guide which you come across online mentions a tendency by the citizens of country xyz to have animated conversations in public and recommends that you should not be bothered by this behaviour. This piece of information might be true, but what do you make of it? You will need to relate it to yourself: if having animated conversations on your mobile phone while commuting to work or university on public transport is normal to you, this behaviour will most likely not be experienced as disruptive when you're abroad. Yet, if you are used to silence or hushed voices when in public, people talking loudly on their mobile phones near you might stress you out. Conversely, if you are used to others joining in spontaneously whenever individual mobile phone conversations are taking place, you might feel that those in country xyz are disinterested in you.

The comparative approach is rooted in the positivist paradigm, that is, the understanding that we can define culture objectively. It mainly employs quantitative research methods. As such, the macro-comparative approach is opposite to the anthropological idea of interpreting micro-cultures in context (Chapter 1), as context is 'small' or 'flowing' within 'fuzzy' demarcation lines, and interpretation as an act of non-objective sensemaking is linked to qualitative methods. Still, both views (Chapter 1 and 2) might enrich each other. This chapter therefore not only presents different cultural dimensions and how they were developed, it also reflects on their usefulness from a cultural perspective. This constitutes another act of interplay, which means to juggle different CCM perspectives and to view them in light of each other in order to look at culture from multiple angles for getting the 'complete picture' (see Introduction).

Early works: comparative anthropology and small-scale methods

Cultural dimensions and comparative CCM emerged out of a process which discarded the original anthropological idea of interpreting 'the whole of micro-culture in context' and by means of longitudinal and ethnographic methods in favour of objectively comparing selected aspects of macro-cultures by means of quantitative methods. The first step towards this development was the emergence of comparative anthropology, which followed from the insight that as culture is 'shared, learned and social', it necessarily implies differences between cultures (as discussed in Chapter 1). The following pages consider this development.

The underlying discussion: what and how to compare?

Cultural dimensions are underpinned by cultural universalism, namely the assumption that all cultures share certain orientations (e.g. a group orientation), and that it is only the degree to which they are character-ized by these orientations which differs, not the underlying cultural concepts themselves (what constitutes a 'group'?).

Cultural universalism has been put forward by British social anthro-pologist E.B. Tylor in order to uncover universal laws of cultural development. Tylor exemplified this approach by comparing the kinship patterns of 350 groups of people (including all kinds of cultural units, from 'tribes' to 'nations') and by identifying universal relations with regard to where to reside and from whom to distance oneself after mar-riage (Tylor, 1889: 245). Tylor's kinship study from 1889 can be considered the first example of comparative cross-cultural research based on cultural universalism. This approach implies that you can 'measure' culture objectively, which is a positivist assumption based on an objectivist worldview (e.g. Hatch with Cunliffe, 2006).

The alternative approach to cultural universalism, called cultural relativism, can be traced back to German-American anthropologist Franz Boas. It argues in favour of studying single cultures and their unique features (Boas, 1896), for example, via participant observation (see Chapter 1). This implies that you cannot study culture 'objectively' but need to find out how groups of people *perceive* the world. This is an interpretative assumption based on an (inter-)subjectivist viewpoint (e.g. Hatch with Cunliffe, 2006). Cultural relativism means, for instance, to acknowledge that you cannot compare the 'Yin-and-Yang-ness' of Brazil versus Mexico because the concept itself is culture-specific to Greater China.

Still, comparisons were made, and when doing so, anthropologists observed that societies seemed to share or combine certain patterns or traits (Schnegg, 2014: 56). Two explanations for this finding were proposed, namely evolutionism and diffusionism: evolutionists argued for a universal human development pattern, diffusionists believed in cultural transmission via migration and trade (Schnegg, 2014: 56).

Since then, the questions of 'what and how to compare' have remained an issue. How to acknowledge culture as 'that complex whole' and still be able to investigate cultural differences and similarities, and their respective roots?

The preliminary answer given to this dilemma was the contrasting comparison of a few cases, for example the works of French sociologist Marcel Mauss on the social significance of gifts (Mauss, 1925). Presumably universal features of culture were distilled from these cases. Mauss, for instance, argued that gifts create a social bond between the giver and receiver. He also proposed that gifts can never be separated from the ones giving and receiving them, and, hence, gifts also tie objects to humans. According to Mauss, gifts serve these two purposes in every culture, regardless of the specifics of the exchange, and this is a culturally-universalist finding.

The work of Clyde Kluckhohn and Fred Strodtbeck

In the 1960s, the small-scale comparative studies of US-American anthropologist Clyde Kluckhohn and social psychologist Fred Strodtbeck (1961) found their way into management, and this is one of the starting points for comparative cross-cultural theory. They draw from longitudinal ethnography and interview-based research among five cultural groups in the Southwest of the USA, among them Navajo Indians and members of The Church of Jesus Christ of Latter-day Saints. Their research was part of a larger interdisciplinary research project on cultural value orientations and led to the identification of six cultural value dimensions and three orientations within each dimension.

First, Kluckhohn and Strodtbeck investigated beliefs about human nature. They ask whether members of a cultural group believe that people are inherently good, mixed or evil. As this question suggests, cultural dimensions cannot be observed directly: they signify invisible cultural meanings which are symbolically expressed in a certain way. It is only via visible expressions of culture that you might infer cultural dimensions. You might then compare their specific configurations across cultures, and, by doing so, gain insights into relative difference.

Kluckhohn and Strodtbeck (1961) also ask the question of how human beings relate to their surroundings, a value dimension which they call 'relationship to nature and environment'. They propose three orientations with regard to this dimension, namely a belief in the need or duty to master nature, to maintain harmony between people and nature, or to subjugate to nature.

This dimension is a good example for how to investigate culture as it relates to you and from an anthropologically-inspired viewpoint, as proposed in the previous chapter. For instance, you could ask yourself what the society you live in is based on. Do you see proof for one or the other value being expressed? How do you live your own life? In which contexts do you live in harmony with nature and how is this expressed? Where and when (and why) do you master your environment?

Still, you will never find absolute proof for one orientation or the other. This is because our lives emerge in a complex interrelation with our environment and nature, and mastery, harmony and subjugation are just three potential shapes which this interrelation might take in a specific context. Additionally, different groups of people have symbolically learned different ways to express an invisible concept such as 'harmony with nature'. We can assume that even though different groups of people might share the orientation 'harmony with nature', they might find different ways of expressing this value and of putting it into social practice. For example, for one group it may mean not killing animals, for another it might require not disturbing the soil by cultivating the land.

The third cultural sphere investigated by Kluckhohn and Strodtbeck (1961) refers to relationships between people. Members of a cultural group might emphasize either the independence of individuals or of nuclear families within a larger group (which suggests an individualistic orientation), consensus within an extended group of equals (which suggests a collateral orientation), or hierarchical principles and deference to higher authorities within the group (which suggests a hierarchical orientation). Again, if you investigate culture at home and apply these orientations broadly, you might find that your life involves all these orientations. For example, you might have grown up in a nuclear family, spent your leisure time among friends which involved making consensus-based decisions among equals, and experienced the hierarchies of work. This suggests that, across all the contexts of your life, you might be able to link yourself to potentially all orientations. Still, in specific contexts, you may have a 'gut feeling' about how to 'normally behave', and these are the cultural glasses we all wear when viewing the world.

For instance, you might have been exposed to just one concept of family in your childhood. So, was it a nuclear family, a larger group of equals, or an extended family with complex hierarchies and a *pater* (or *mater*) *familias*? If it was a nuclear family, this may well be the concept of family which you carry on instinctively. Of course, you will make new experiences, adapt and refine the concept and add new items to your cultural backpack. But still, the nuclear family might feel the most natural, and alternative orientations might remain a 'blind spot'. To overcome this blind spot, you could investigate the contexts of your life wherein you have experienced alternative orientations. For instance, extended hierarchical families might be similar to hierarchies you have encountered at work, and you could proceed from this initial link in order to understand alternative concepts of family. Still, given the tacit and implicit nature of cultural knowledge and meaning, this act obviously has its limits: another concept of family might not 'feel' the same, on an instinctive, emotional, behavioural and perceived level, for it requires a conscious act of transference. Nonetheless, any initial link is a suitable starting point for grasping an alternative cultural meaning.

Besides orientations towards environment, nature and other human beings, Kluckhohn and Strodtbeck also investigated concepts of time. They asked whether members of a cultural group believe that people should make decisions with respect to events in the past, events in the present, or events in the future. These orientations are labelled past, present and future orientation. Again, in your own life, you might have experienced all of these. However, you may not have pursued each in every context.

This can also be said for the fifth cultural orientation, namely the nature of human activity. It refers to whether members of a cultural group believe that people should live for the moment (being), should aim for personal growth as defined by personal beliefs (being-in-becoming), or should focus on achieving goals which are defined externally (doing/achieving). For instance, if success at work is measured through visible material achievements such as a house, a car, etc., this signifies a 'doing' orientation. Still, the same person aiming at these material gains might only work as much as is needed to finance them; afterwards, they might refrain from a 'doing' orientation and focus more on 'being'. This means that cultural orientations might change over time and across contexts or as soon as specific goals have been achieved – even within one individual. This suggests that cultural orientations are unlikely to be experienced in their 'purest' form: they are theoretical constructs after all, and culture and life are much more complicated. Still, you have to start your cultural investigation somewhere, and cultural orientations are a good point of departure for becoming aware of the symbolic meanings attached to certain visible facets of culture.

Kluckhohn and Strodtbeck also investigated conceptions of space, namely the question as to whether members of a cultural group believe that space should belong to individuals, that space should belong to all, or that the distribution of space should be a combination thereof. They labelled these orientations as private, public and mixed conceptions of space. For the study of culture and CCM, this dimension is significant, as it reminds us that culture goes beyond individual interaction, knowledge, meaning and behaviour, and involves material objects and concepts of 'what the world should be like', and how to organize space is one aspect of implementing a certain worldview.

This suggests that we not only need to pay attention to how people do things around here or there and how they give meaning to the world, but that we also need to include what their world 'looks like'. For instance, when travelling across countries and regions, you might notice differences in the degree to which individuals live in houses with private gardens and as to whether their lawn is fenced and/or shielded from view by hedges or walls. You may also observe that it is more common for children to play on the streets or in a public playground than in a private garden and vice versa. Most likely, you will find patterns in these differences, which suggests a cultural root to them, yet the cultural level from which this pattern originates might be unclear (regional? local? societal? etc.). It could also be that some lawns look different or change their appearance over time. So, culture also encompasses exceptions and change.

Reflections on research methods and their outcome

For understanding the outcome of cultural research, it is essential to become aware of its methods. As Chapter 1 suggests, it is a major limitation of interview-based cultural research that it cannot uncover non-verbal, non-cognitive and tacit culture. One of the strengths of Kluckhohn and Strodtbeck's (1961) research is that they (mainly Clyde Kluckhohn) did not only rely on interviews but also employed ethnographic methods. Via participant observation, they were able to trace culture over time and across different individuals, and the cultures studied were small and few enough to be 'experienced' by the researcher.

Despite the virtues of ethnography, the mere complexity of the task (how to compare cultures?) meant that small-scale comparative studies based on longitudinal and in-depth methods gave way to other methods, mainly language-based research, which was related to the level of macro-cultures, with the above-mentioned limitations. This shift led to the creation of intercultural communication and comparative CCM as distinct CCM approaches, as we will see below.

Intercultural communication and its specific training context

Originally trained as an anthropologist, US-American Edward Twitchell Hall Jr is one of the founding figures of intercultural communication as a discipline.

The Foreign Service Institute and its practical demands

When developing his theories, Hall worked for the US State Department, teaching intercultural communication skills at the Foreign Service Institute (FSI). This was originally a language-training institute for US diplomats and selected army staff.[1] It was founded in 1946 with the goal to increase the effectiveness of the American Foreign Service abroad (Leeds-Hurwitz, 1990: 264).

It was at the FSI that the field of intercultural communication emerged in its specific configuration, and according to US-American communication scholar Wendy Leeds-Hurwitz, who has traced this development, Hall was one of the major actors in this process (Leeds-Hurwitz, 1990: 262). Still, according to her, establishing a new discipline was secondary to 'Hall's early attempt to translate anthropological insights into cultural differences to an audience that wanted immediate and practical results' (Leeds-Hurwitz, 1990: 262). As a result, intercultural communication emerged as a *training* discipline, based on the assumed need to develop intercultural communication skills for their practical application (Pusch, 2004: 15).

Today, intercultural communication skills, intercultural competencies, 'doing business in country xyz' are indeed standard seminars offered by numerous intercultural trainers in many companies around the world, and corporate human resource departments measure the success of these activities (Szkudlarek, 2009). Such developments can be viewed as a direct outcome of Hall's work (Leeds-Hurwitz, 1990: 263–264), and we will critically examine these in Chapters 4 and 5.

Approaching selected interaction patterns with linguistic models

To deliver the practical results demanded for by his students, Hall shifted from analysing the whole of culture ('that complex whole') to the analysis of selected interaction patterns between representatives of different cultures (Leeds-Hurwitz, 1990: 263). Particularly, Hall approached culture with models borrowed from descriptive linguistics. This approach is epitomized in the statement 'Culture is communication and communication is culture' (E.T., Hall, 1959: 186).

When focusing on communication, Hall (1959, 1966, 1976, 1983) understood it as encompassing more than language and as including, for instance, tone of voice, gestures, density of communication, context, time, and concepts and usage of space. Standard intercultural training scenarios, such as first-contact situations, business behaviour and nego- tiation skills, are implicit in Hall's work (see Chapter 3). In line with this intention, I will partly present Hall's concepts from an applied intercultural training perspective in what follows.

Descriptive linguistics analyses how language is actually used by a group of people or speech community. Different categories of communi- cation are considered, such as verbal, non-verbal (body language, gestures, etc.) and para-verbal (e.g. tone, pitch and pacing of the voice, and wider contextual factors). Hall applied these concepts to the analysis of intercultural interactions. For example, in a conversation, speakers might be used to more or less conversational overlap between individual statements, which is a facet of para-verbal communication. A classic intercultural training example is a statement by the trainer such as 'Finnish speakers are used to less conversational overlap than Spanish speakers. Therefore, a Finn might feel interrupted by a Spaniard (because s/he seems to "jump into the conversation too quickly"), whereas the Spanish person will most likely get the impression that the Finnish person is disinterested in the conversation (for s/he seems "too slow to react").'

Hall (1966) also focused on proxemics, our culturally-informed percep- tions and usages of space. For instance, it might happen that members of different cultures keep more or less of a speaking distance. When interacting interculturally, they might then feel uncomfortable in the presence of others, either feeling disregarded (perception of too much distance) or beset (perception of insufficient distance). Awareness of proxemics might therefore help them identify and describe perceived cross-cultural differences and become aware of their origins.

Another theme in Hall's (1983) work is perceptions of time: a monochronic cultural orientation implies dividing time into several time slots and allocating specific activities to each time slot which are then carried out one after the other. A polychronic cultural orientation is linked to not apportioning time and managing different activities which are carried out in parallel. In my own intercultural training practice, I used the pictures of 'keeping time' and 'juggling with time' to exemplify these orientations. These aspects remind us that communication, in its cultural sense, is much more than language and spoken words; it involves tacit and pre-reflexive assumptions on space, time, silence, and so on, and to stress this point is a major contribution of Hall's work.

Communication and context

Hall (1966) describes several aspects regarding the style and focus of communication. According to him, communication might tend to neglect context (low-context) or take context into account (high-context). At this point, we need to note that his definition of context *only* refers to selected surrounding factors of an interactional context, namely those which are relevant to his theory of culture as communication. It does not equal the anthropological understanding of context which is used throughout this book (see Chapter 1).

Following Hall (1966), low-context communication is largely direct, verbal and explicit, whereas high-context communication is largely indirect, non-verbal and implicit. Low-context orientation implies a focus on language and the words spoken, high-context means 'speaking and reading between the lines', for which more than verbal signs are relevant. You could simplify low-context as 'listen to what I say (and only to what I say)' and high-context as 'listen to what I don't say'. In my own intercultural training practice, I have compared low-context to a German-style speedway or 'autobahn': no speed limit, fast driving, the focus solely on the road; however, you might be stressed out afterwards. Conversely, high-context might be pictured as a winding country road: it is the overall experience that counts, the focus on the landscape, and you may not reach your destination quickly (which is also not the purpose of the drive).

According to Hall (1966), each communication style is related to the speed and complexity of the information expressed and perceived: whereas low-context communication is linked to fast and simple information, high-context implies slow and complex information. In my own intercultural training practice, I have referred to low-context information as catching fish with a fishing rod: you aim at specific fish and you can only catch one fish at a time; in order to be successful, you need to know where to find the right kind of fish. Acquiring or interpreting high-context information is a bit like catching fish with a net: you throw a net over the whole pond, and when tightening it, you get an overview on all the kinds of fish available. This implies that you gather complex information holistically, and it is only afterwards that this information is sorted. A net might be suitable for unknown situations wherein the question to be asked remains unclear (as is often the case in CCM). Still, this requires time and patience, and multiple interactions.

High-context orientation also implies the differentiation between in-group and out-group. Those who are similar to or affiliated with the sender of the message in a certain way are members of the in-group and possess a higher contextual knowledge for deciphering it. Those other members of society (out-groups) who are different from the immediate in-group or not affiliated with the sender in a certain way might lack this ability. This involves a fine and complex web of status-related inter-dependencies. The more different two individuals are (in terms of in- and out-group relations), the more difficult it might become to convey negative messages, especially if you need to communicate up the hierarchy. The tricky part, at least to an outsider, is to understand which kind of difference counts for making this differentiation. You can best think of in-group and out-group differentiation as the understanding that society or an organization is a chest with many drawers: if you share a drawer with someone else – that is, if you have sufficiently much in common – you are in-group; if not, you are out-group. This also implies that you need to know the person responsible for a certain drawer (the key or 'box opener'), and in order to soften the difficulties of having to communicate across boxes, you might approach the box-opener first, preferably informally, and consider the above-mentioned web of social relations.

Often, high-context communication has been described as the opposite of low-context information. However, at least to my mind, context-oriented communication (high-context) includes a variety of styles, depending on the context. Conversely, low-context communication tends not to vary much across contexts; it is not so much 'direct' but rather 'blunt'. From my experience, 'direct' communication contexts in a highly context-oriented environment are often 'backstage' (at the coffee machine as opposed to at a meeting) and in-group (towards well-known colleagues and without too much difference in hierarchies and interests). High-context is also different from indirectness: it simply means that the decision of how to communicate is based on assessments of the factors influencing interaction, such as: who is present? How well do we know each other? Do I need to convey a positive or negative message? Low-context, on the other hand, tends to neglect these wider factors, focusing mainly on the message itself.

For instance, imagine that you are an expert in a certain topic and need to present a negative status report to higher management in a formal meeting wherein customer representatives and many other 'boxes' are present. Let's now think of the message as something 'smelly'. Which decision are you going to make now? Are you going to convey your negative message right now, which implies that you step into the 'smelly stuff', and the whole meeting will stink? Or do you inform the most relevant addressee one-to-one in front of the coffee machine and simply convey a softened message during the meeting so that the smell is contained? Or, if you feel that you cannot deliver the message to the actual addressee directly, will you approach them via a suitable intermediary so that you are not the one to force the smell upon them?

Whenever they communicate, individuals need to decide what to focus on: the negative content of the message (low-context) or its positive wrapping based on their assessment of what the context requires (high-context). This decision depends on what matters more: saying it 'as it is' or containing the smell. Still, in every style, it is possible to deliver bad news: it is going to stink somewhere, and also in high-context, but it should not stink everywhere, for a complex web of social relations needs to be maintained. From a low-context perspective, the differences in statements across contexts which are associated with a high-context orientation might not seem trustworthy; from a high-context perspective, it is the bluntness of low-communication messages (it stinks everywhere!) which are hard to bear. Those oriented towards low-context, however, don't focus on the smell (and therefore remain insensitive to it).

Reflections on underlying changes in theory and method

The interdisciplinary link between anthropology and linguistics, as put forward by Hall, created the field of intercultural communication and facilitated intercultural training practice. Many of Hall's concepts, with the foremost being high- and low-context orientation, have become standard intercultural training tools. Implicit to his work is the under-standing that we need to differentiate between how something is 'meant' from the inside and 'perceived' from the outside (Leeds-Hurwitz, 1990: 264), and we will come back to this thought in Chapter 3.

Hall also introduced important shifts to the discipline. In contrast to Kluckhohn and Strodtbeck (1961), who study 'the whole' of several small-scale cultures holistically and over a longer period of time, Hall focuses only on selected units of culture as relevant to his concept of intercultural interactions, but draws implications for macro-cultures, such as nations and society, comparing, for example, US-Americans and Japanese. Furthermore, due to Hall's specific focus of work at the FSI, US-American 'culture' and 'US-Americans being abroad' are the implicit points of reference for much of his writing. His cultural dimensions are bipolar, meaning that you can only have one orientation or the other in an intercultural interaction context.

Kluckhohn and Strodtbeck's orientations, on the other hand, also allow for variance *within* cultures, within individuals and across differ-ent contexts and points in time. To them, it is the individual who carries or acquires a certain orientation, and it is only when the individual is viewed in relation to others of the same or different groups that cultural patterns emerge (Maznevski et al., 2002).

Hall's studies can therefore be considered half-way between prior small-scale comparative ethnography and the large-scale research on numerous macro-cultures which we will encounter in the following sub-section. The principle of bipolar cultural orientations ('either–or') already shows up in Hall's work but will manifest itself more strongly in the works of Dutch social psychologist and comparative CCM 'guru' Geert Hofstede. To fully understand how to use this tool, we will there-fore need to move to large-scale quantitative studies, mainly the work of Hofstede and project GLOBE (House et al., 2004).

The shift towards bipolar opposites: from Hofstede to project GLOBE

Geert Hofstede's (1980, 2001, 2010; Hofstede and Bond, 1988) can be considered the most widely used comparative cross-cultural framework in theory and practice. Referring back to earlier work, Hofstede devel-oped six cultural dimensions over the course of several years, namely power distance, uncertainty avoidance, individualism versus collectivism, masculinity versus femininity, long-term versus short-term orientation, and indulgence versus restraint.

Cultural dimensions as an 'either–or': the example of indulgence versus restraint

Hofstede's study redefined comparative theory in a way that has dominated the discipline ever since. Specifically, it presented culture by means of bipolar opposites, implying an 'either–or' orientation. To give an example for this paradigmatic shift, Hofstede's (2010) dimension 'indulgence versus restraint' describes the degree to which individuals receive social gratification of basic human desires versus the degree to which a society controls this gratification. Let's now say you want to find out more about the US-American lifestyle. From the perspective of Kluckhohn and Strodtbeck (1961), US-American work-life seems to involve a strong 'doing' orientation, as individuals tend to work hard in order to finance a certain lifestyle. At the same time, you can also deduce a 'being orientation' from the observation that someone might stop working hard as soon as they have achieved certain goals. Internal variance across time and contexts is not only possible, but also to be expected. Conversely, Hofstede's cultural dimensions are opposites aggregated across all contexts and individuals and fixed in time. This makes US-American culture an 'indulgent' culture on the Hofstede scale (The Hofstede Centre, 2016a) which is opposite to those countries orienting themselves towards 'restraint'.

Two studies in light of each other: the example of performance orientation

When discussing Hofstede's dimensions in the following, I will do so in light of project GLOBE (House et al., 2004), which can be linked back to Hofstede's work. The GLOBE (Global Leadership and Organizational Behaviour Effectiveness) study is the most recent large-scale comparative CCM study. It has received attention mainly in academia. Its nine cultural dimensions are based on data from various cultures which were collected by 170 scholars who conducted more than 17,000 interviews with middle managers from 62 countries in three industries (House et al., 2004). In comparison to GLOBE, the database of Hofstede's four initial dimensions seems narrow: they originate from employee survey data collected between 1967 and 1973 in a single multinational company (IBM). Hofstede's approach has therefore been critiqued for confusing organizational with national culture (P. Smith, 2006). On the other hand, the GLOBE study's design has also been questioned, for instance, by Hofstede (2006) himself.

In contrast to Hofstede's sole focus on national cultures, project GLOBE differentiated between societal and organizational culture.

It analysed societies instead of nations, and some nations were split up into different societal clusters in order to account for inner-societal diversity. GLOBE societal clusters are, for instance, English-speaking and French-speaking Canada, former East and former West Germany, and White and non-White South Africa. Furthermore, GLOBE differentiated between cultural practices and values. Interviewees were asked, for example, to evaluate their actual cultural practices – 'as is' – and the level of cultural values – 'should be'. The intention was to uncover potential gaps between cultural reality and cultural ideal, and these gaps might be significant for investigating culture. For example, interviewees of all cultures rated gender inequality to be existent ('as is') but also stated the need to minimize it ('should be') (Javidan, House and Dorfman, 2004: 29).

GLOBE's and Hofstede's work are interlinked. GLOBE proposes the nine cultural dimensions of power distance, uncertainty avoidance, in-group collectivism, institutional collectivism, assertiveness, humane orientation, gender egalitarianism, future orientation and performance orientation (House and Javidan, 2004: 11–14; Javidan, House and Dorfman, 2004: 30). The last one, performance orientation, refers to the degree to which a society or organization encourages and rewards group members for performance improvement and excellence. The Hofstede dimension indulgence versus restraint was published in 2010, and might have been informed by it. On the other hand, several GLOBE dimensions refer back to Hofstede's first four dimensions, namely power distance, uncertainty avoidance, individualism versus collectivism and masculinity versus femininity, which were first published in 1980.

Due to the fact that GLOBE explicitly refers back to Hofstede and that Hofstede responded to GLOBE (Hofstede, 2006), and also because of a heated academic discussion for and against Hofstede or GLOBE (e.g. P. Smith, 2006), it makes sense to view both studies in light of each other.

Power distance and uncertainty avoidance

Power distance and uncertainty avoidance are concepts by Hofstede (1980), but remain more or less unchanged in the GLOBE study. Power distance refers to the degree to which members of a cultural group expect and accept an unequal distribution of power. Uncertainty avoidance refers to the degree to which a group of people feels uncomfortable when facing uncertainty and ambiguity. Using the term 'group' is my own doing, based on the understanding that culture emerges on multiple levels (Hofstede refers to 'nations'; GLOBE to societal and organizational cultures).

Individuals with a 'high uncertainty avoidance', that is those who wish to counteract the unpredictability of future events, might do so in different ways. For example, you can alleviate the uncertainty of project management by detailed task-oriented planning or you can do so by establishing a proper network of individuals who might help the project along in the future. Low certainty avoidance does not imply that a person does not care about future events, but rather that they *accept* not being able to control the risks associated with these events. From an intercultural training perspective, you might think of low uncertainty avoidance as an outlook which perceives life as a roll of the dice: sometimes we lose, and sometimes we win, and we cannot fully predict the outcome of our actions. Conversely, high uncertainty avoidance might mean looking at life as a single game of chess, wherein moves are planned and their consequences are being pondered over well in advance.

From my point of view, the purpose of this and other dimensions is not to categorize others but to reflect upon what influences our own behaviour and perceptions. In my own intercultural training practice, I introduced these dimensions mainly to create awareness with regard to our own cultural backpacks. I experienced that individuals tended to find that they had experienced different orientations in different contexts, or, in the words of an Indian participant during one of my training sessions, that they had played 'backgammon' as a combination of playing chess and rolling dice.

Individualism versus collectivism

Hofstede's concept 'individualism versus collectivism' describes the degree to which members of a group put forward their own interests against the group and hold self-reliance to be valuable (individualism) versus the degree to which members of a group align their interests with those of the group and consider this valuable (collectivism). It can be linked to Kluckhohn and Strodtbeck's (1961) differentiation between individualistic, collateral and hierarchical relationships.

Individualism does not imply that you are not integrated into a larger whole: everyone is somehow. Still, the notion of what 'being in a team' *means* might differ. For Hofstede's understanding of individualism, you can picture individual track and field athletes who are awarded a team medal. For collectivism, you might imagine individuals rowing together in a boat. The former will try to jump as high, run as fast, etc. as s/he can individually, and it is the outcome of individual excellence that forms a team. The latter will try to synchronize their efforts (it can even be harmful if a single member rows too fast) and they will follow the advice of a collective pace-maker for doing so.

Project GLOBE critiqued Hofstede's approach as mixing up internal and external motivations for being or becoming part of a group. Consecutively, GLOBE divided collectivism into two aspects: institutional and in-group collectivism. Institutional collectivism refers to the degree to which organizational and societal institutional practices encourage and reward the collective distribution of resources and action. In-group collectivism describes the degree to which individuals express pride, loyalty, and cohesiveness in their organizations or families. In summary, GLOBE differentiates between the external encouragement of group orientation and the inner motivation to orient the individual self towards groups. For instance, individuals might be highly competitive at work, and for encouraging stronger group orientation, organizations might offer team-based incentives (institutional collectivism). Or individuals might prefer to work in groups, and team-work might be a quasi-natural outcome of their intrinsic motivation (in-group collectivism).

Masculinity versus femininity and its critique

Hofstede's next dimension, masculinity versus femininity, encompasses two aspects (Hofstede, 2001: 312). First, a masculine business style implies the dominance of values that are considered 'masculine', such as assertiveness and competitiveness. In contrast, a 'feminine' business style implies the dominance of values that are considered 'feminine', such as care, cooperation and modesty. As a consequence, Hofstede assumes societies with masculine business styles to be dominated by men, and the business spheres of societies with a feminine business style to have more gender equality in business. This mixture makes this dimension a suitable example for reflecting upon the fact that cultural dimensions are products of the time and the cultural context wherein they emerge: when Hofstede developed his concept of masculinity and femininity based on data gathered between 1967 and 1972, gender stereotypes were part of everyday social interactions in many societies. To complicate matters, his data originate from a single company, namely IBM, and on a methodological level we might wonder how many women actually worked at IBM in the 1960s and 1970s.

Critical diversity studies have by now highlighted the nature of gender as a culture-specific social construction (Acker, 2012). This implies that men are not born competitive and assertive, and women are not born cooperative and modest. Rather, they might have socially learned to *be* a certain way, thereby internalizing culturally-informed gender roles. Additionally, as we still may observe today, academic, social, economic and political power in many countries tends to rest in the hands of men. This might result in notable gender-based differences in cultural perceptions, as, for example, GLOBE suggests: whereas male managers tend to believe that their own society provides equal opportunities and has already advanced the rights of women, female managers tend to doubt this across *all* the countries studied (Javidan, House and Dorfman, 2004: 29). Labelling certain culturally-learned ways of doing things as 'masculine' and 'feminine', and equalling 'masculinity' with male dominance in business under such conditions, might perpetuate such gender stereotyping (Emrich, Denmark and Den Hartog, 2004; House and Javidan, 2004: 13–14).

Assertiveness, gender egalitarianism and humane orientation

To overcome these limitations, GLOBE divided Hofstede's concept of masculinity into two aspects. The first aspect refers to the expected business style. A high degree to which a 'masculine' business style (in Hofstede terminology) is expected has been re-labelled 'high assertiveness' (House and Javidan, 2004: 13–14). A high degree to which a 'feminine' business style is expected has been re-named 'low assertiveness'. The equality of males and females in societies has been termed 'gender egalitarianism'.

It is important to note that the 'new' GLOBE dimension of 'humane orientation' does not equal Hofstede's 'femininity' and does not constitute the opposite of 'assertiveness'. Rather, humane orientation refers to the degree to which a society or organization encourages and rewards individuals for being fair, altruistic, generous, caring, and kind to others. It intends to capture the institutionalized aspects of caring for each other. With this dimension, GLOBE tried to take previously neglected concepts of social obligations into account, referring – among others – to Kluckhohn and Strodtbeck's (1961) understanding of relations between people.

Long-term versus short-term orientation and its critique

In 1988 (Hofstede and Bond), Hofstede introduced a fifth dimension, namely long-term orientation versus short-term orientation, which was based on survey research conducted in 23 countries. Long-term orientation implies that members of a group pay attention to status differences and value seniority, have a strong work ethic and perseverance, and respect tradition. Short-term orientation implies that members of a group do not place a high priority on status, try to postpone old age, are concerned with short-term results and aim for quick satisfaction of needs. This dimension can be linked to Kluckhohn and Strodtbeck's (1961) concept of past, present and future orientation, and to the work of Bulgarian sociologist Michael Minkov (2007). With this dimension, Hofstede and Bond (1988) try to take specific Confucian values into account; they also refer to it as 'Confucian work dynamism'.

GLOBE questioned the presumed link of 'long-term versus short-term orientation' to Confucian values (Ashkanasy et al., 2004: 282–342), yet retained other aspects of this dimension. It was renamed 'future orientation', defined as the extent to which individuals engage in future-oriented behaviour such as delaying gratification, planning and investing in the future. In any case, I am not sure whether it is actually possible to trace ancient philosophical thought to today's managerial world (imagine having to give an answer to questions such as 'how can I see Christian/Jewish/Muslim/Buddhist value orientations in the way projects are typically managed around here?').

Alternative and non-comparative macro-level studies

Cultural dimensions by Fons Trompenaars and Charles Hampden-Turner

Obviously, Hofstede and project GLOBE are not the only large-scale comparative CCM studies. On a more applied level, Hofstede's work has, for instance, been carried on by Dutch-French economist, organizational researcher and interculturalist Fons Trompenaars (1993). Together with British management scholar Charles Hampden-Turner (1997), he conducted another large-scale study of culture which identified opposing pairs of value orientations based on a questionnaire that had been distributed to managers from 28 countries over a period of ten years. Subsequently, it was applied to a much larger number of countries, including the former Soviet Bloc which had not been part of Hofstede's database (there was no IBM in the Soviet Union at that time). This research resulted in seven cultural dimensions, some of which introduce new angles and are mentioned here.

Trompenaars' and Hampden-Turner's (1997) 'universalism versus particularism' is similar to Hall's (1966) low- and high-context orientation.

It refers to the degree to which members of a cultural group treat every-one equally and favour one rule or norm for all situations (universalism) or to which members of a cultural group treat groups of people differ-ently, for example based on relations, and favour many context-specific norms (particularism). You could best picture 'universalism versus par-ticularism' as the answer to the question of what makes a 'good rule or guideline': is it that the 'good rule' should be generalizable and apply to all situations, regardless of the circumstances (universalism), or is it that the 'good rule' is the one that fits a specific context in the best possible way, which implies that there is no single good rule (particularism)?

Drawing from Hall's (1966) notion of spatial relations, Trompenaars and Hampden-Turner (1997) also proposed that concepts of relation-ships as linked to specific spheres of life might differ across cultures: specific relationships are characterized by a separation of personal and public spheres. This implies that the private sphere is reserved for close friends and family and is not to be touched upon in public, e.g. at work. Relationships are diffuse if each sphere can be touched upon, and especially so in a public context, and if there is no clear and reli-able process for moving from one sphere to the other. For example, if you differentiate between friends and acquaintances in your life, this suggests that you are oriented towards specific relationships. A classic intercultural training example is a US-American manager inviting a German colleague to their home (most likely in a casual 'and whenever you are in the vicinity, please *do* come and visit us' way), and the German manager interpreting this not as diffuse politeness but as a specific personal invitation.

Trompenaars and Hampden-Turner (1997) also asked the ques-tion as to whether status at work is ascribed, for instance based on family background or titles, or achieved by proven competency. This dimension points to differences with regard to how to 'see' and be assured of another person's competency at work. For instance, the management of engineering projects is a crucial task. But who is the right kind of person for the job? Should you have gained practical experience in engineering management or should you have the right kind of degree? And what is the right kind of degree, anyway? As these questions suggest, it makes sense to reflect upon culturally-relative assumptions regarding 'who is perceived as competent and why', and concepts such as achieved versus ascribed status might be an initial trigger point for doing so. Another potentially helpful dimension by Trompenaars and Hampden-Turner (1997) is affectiv-ity versus neutrality, which refers to the degree to which emotions are (not) shown or (not) acceptable.

Further studies

Ultimately, most cultural dimensions or orientations are linked to each other, and therefore this overview only discussed those studies which triggered or commented upon major shifts. If you wish to learn more, you can find, for instance, further frameworks of value orientations and cultural dimensions (e.g. Triandis, 1994, 1995; Minkov, 2007, 2011), some at an organizational level (Schein, 1985), and not all of them based on bipolar orientations (Schwartz, 1992, 1994). Additionally, practitioners have introduced alternative training models (e.g. R.D. Lewis, 1996, 2012).

Non-comparative approaches

Having said all this about comparative studies, I also need to mention that not all of macro-level CCM research is comparative. Some scholars try to capture what you could broadly call 'cultural essence' (Holden, 2002: 25), that is something like the national character, a societal value orientation, cultural norms, and so on. For instance, US-American management scholars Michael Gannon and Rajnandini Pillai (2010) proposed that culture can be investigated via metaphors, such as 'the Spanish bullfight' or 'the Turkish coffeehouse'. From their viewpoint, the whole of culture unfolds from these metaphors.

Alternatively, German psychologist Alexander Thomas (Thomas, Kinast and Schroll-Machl, 2003a, 2003b) has focused on so-called Kulturstandards ('culture standards'), which are standards or norms for national cultures (also see Romani, Primecz and Topçu, 2011). Based on Thomas's work and making it accessible to an English-speaking audience, German intercultural psychologist Sylvia Schroll-Machl (2003) identifies the following Kulturstandards for Germany: objectivism; appreciation for rules, regulations and standards; rule-oriented, internalized control; time planning; separation of personality and living spheres; separation of professional and private; a low-context communication style; and individualism. As this rather abstract list suggests, Kulturstandards, too, need to be contextualized in order to deliver meaningful advice, and we will discuss the requirements for doing so below.

These non-comparative works proceed from a culturally-relative perspective; however, they still focus on macro-level culture. For example, the investigation of identity and alternative levels of difference, such as perceived conflict between management and workers or between members of different ethnicities, tends to be covered by management and organization studies or by diversity research and not by CCM. Still, and for reasons which I will discuss in Chapter 4, I think that CCM *should* concern itself with these issues.

How (not) to use this tool: cultural dimensions in managerial practice

Applying cultural dimensions to CCM practice starts with the awareness of how this tool has developed, and how the theoretical assumptions and methods underpinning specific studies influence their outcome, benefits and limitations. To my mind, the business-etiquette approach is how *not* to use cultural dimensions (or non-comparative macro-level tools such as Kulturstandards), whereas the ethnographic frame of mind enables us to combine the strengths of the micro-cultural and the macro-cultural/comparative cross-cultural perspective.

The need for theoretical and methodological awareness

As the previous considerations suggest, the nature of cross-cultural research changed over time. Early works were linked to anthropological theories and methods and investigated culture holistically. Starting with Hall, culture was increasingly simplified, as were the methods for studying it. To cite a CCM insight from Hall (1976: 17), 'Americans overseas are psychologically stressed in many ways when confronted by P-time [polychronic time] systems such as those in Latin America and the Middle East'. As this quote suggests, Hall assumes that individuals share certain orientations on the level of societies or even larger geographical units, and he assumes these macro-level differences to manifest themselves in intercultural micro-level interactions. However, from an anthropologically-inspired cultural perspective (see Chapter 1), specific micro-contexts cannot be prescribed in such a rigid manner.

From Hofstede onwards, comparative cross-cultural research meant large-scale macro-level studies which relied on language-based methods such as interviews, questionnaires and surveys. This suggests that explicit culture was favoured over tacit culture (see Chapter 1). Findings were presented by means of bipolar opposites, implying an 'either–or' orientation, and the borders between cultures were fixed on the societal and national level, and also studies refraining from direct comparison depart from the dictum of presumed macro-cultural difference.

Such a categorical and generalized approach to culture has severe shortcomings. Think of multi-ethnic, multicultural and multi-lingual nations such as Indonesia or India, or the Basque region as a cultural and linguistic cluster across national borders. In the Hofstede study or project GLOBE, India would just be a single culture and the Basque region would be subsumed under either France or Spain.

The change from in-depth studies of 'the whole of culture' in several micro-cultures to language-based survey research in numerous macro-cultures also brings about methodological questions, such as: How can we be sure that the cultural orientations of single individuals are representative of a whole society, organization or nation? Is it possible at all to investigate largely tacit cultural elements via explicit (language-based) methods? How can we understand those facets of CCM which are beyond communication and rational thought, and which involve objects and technology? How can we make sure not to confuse organizational culture, managerial roles and many more micro-contextual factors with national culture?

Nonetheless: the benefits of cultural dimensions

Still, if we reflect upon cultural dimensions *as a concept*, many seem to 'make sense', and I have tried to share my thoughts on this matter when discussing them. Conversely, using them as *prescriptions* might not do justice to complex reality and the cross-cultural tasks at hand.

Having said this, I would still like to propose the following benefits of cultural dimensions. First, they give cultural orientations a name-tag, thereby making features of tacit culture explicit. Secondly, they enable us to understand that struggles in interpersonal interactions might simply be a result of different collective orientations (and not an individual nuisance or a purposeful 'sabotage' from the other person's side). This realization might help us to exchange our perceptions of each other's ways of doing things without making it personal. Finally, cultural dimensions could be useful for understanding how each and every one of us is a product and producer of culture, for – once we are aware of them – we tend to 'see' them in our own doings and perceptions of the world.

In summary, and due to their simplicity, cultural dimensions are *the* initial tool for pinpointing cultural differences and making them comprehensive.

Managerial realities (I) and the 'business-etiquette approach'

We can observe that Hofstede's work, particularly his first four dimensions, has become the most influential comparative cross-cultural study. Its success is most likely due to the fact that he proposed quantifiable indices by which nations are ranked. Indices based on his dimensions are easily accessible on the internet and can be downloaded as smartphone applications. Online tools for immediate comparison are available as well: the ideal tool for a fast-paced, key-performance-indicators-monitoring and globally-interconnected business world, it might seem.

Just imagine this practical scenario. Your employer informs you of the need to travel to country xyz tomorrow in order to conduct joint venture negotiations of the utmost importance. You have never been to country xyz and have just this evening to prepare. You know that your next step up the managerial ladder will depend on the outcome of these negotiations. Grooming you for this next step, your employer had even paid for you to attend an in-house international negotiation skills seminar provided by an intercultural training agency. By now, your superiors and the corporate human resource (HR) department will expect that you know 'how to negotiate across cultures'; this was a defined learning goal of the seminar you attended (naturally, the seminar has been certified by HR to make sure that the intended outcome is delivered by the intercultural training agency). In summary: your knowledge of 'how to do it' is presumably 'guaranteed'.

Still, you have a problem: country xyz was not covered in the seminar, it is not a big customer market, not one of those everyone rushes into these days. You are still lost and need to prepare. Anything solid, some statistics and a few guidelines would be a lifesaver right now. So you browse the internet, and there they are: Hofstede's cultural dimensions and how certain countries score with regard to them (The Hofstede Centre, 2016b). You can compare the scores for your home country abc and your destination xyz; the higher the score, the higher the preference for a cultural dimension in a particular country. You click twice, and you have a comparison: the PDI (power distance index) for country xyz is 69 as compared to 11 in country abc (your home country); on the other hand, country abc is high on uncertainty avoidance: its UAI (uncertainty avoidance index) is 68 (in contrast to a UAI of 23 in country xyz). Suddenly, the principle of relative difference has become quantifiable. Still, this information does not seem specific enough. What does it *mean* for the task at hand? You browse again, and find a business etiquette webpage. It states, for example, how people in country xyz conduct business, what kind of hierarchy they expect, and how to give and receive business cards, etc. Just what you need right now! Relieved, you pack your bag and drive to the airport with the comforting feeling that you will land the next morning 'prepared'.

Unfortunately, the business etiquette guideline approach – even though it might ease managerial anxiety – neglects the nature of culture as changing, paradoxical and context-specific. It also does not allow for reflexivity regarding your own cultural backpack, and these two aspects – how I have learned to do things and how I perceive the doings of others – are inevitably linked. Just imagine that the business etiquette webpage also offers information on your home country abc. It says (I am anonymizing an existing webpage here), 'Country abc people try to avoid uncertainty and plan everything carefully. Country abc is a society that relies on laws, rules and regulation. In business, country abc people reduce risks to the minimum and proceed step by step'. Being an 'abc person' yourself, you will most likely feel misrepresented at this point, and reject this statement as being too simplistic and stereotypical. Still, when under pressure to perform, there might be a tendency to approach others (xyz people) this way. Therefore, business etiquette guidelines are an omnipresent danger in CCM practice (and sometimes in research and education as well).

Managerial realities (II) and the ethnographic frame of mind

Cultural dimensions present relative difference – and some of them, such as Hofstede and project GLOBE, even in a quantifiable and statistical manner – yet we cannot translate these findings into reality one-to-one. As aggregated, static and macro-level concepts, what cultural dimensions fail to do is predict individual behaviour, trace culture across contexts and time, or explain the whole of specific interactions. Using them as prescriptions is a clear misapplication of the concept. It might result in generalized and absolute beliefs about others, that is, stereotypes. These stereotypes might be disguised as knowledge, but they still remain what they are: somewhat 'sophisticated' stereotypes (see also Osland and Bird, 2000). Therefore, and despite the previous considerations, the question remains: how to use this tool? The prescriptive business etiquette guideline is one way to go – but the wrong one, at least from a critical, reflexive and culturally-aware viewpoint. As a more valuable alternative, I would therefore like to propose the ethnographic frame of mind (inspired by Barbara Czarniawska's 1998 'anthropological frame of mind').

Let me explain the ethnographic frame of mind with the help of an example, which again is related to the CCM scenario of being sent abroad for negotiations the next day. Let's say that this scenario now refers to a male German manager from the German subsidiary of a French multinational company, who is being sent to Taiwan by his French superior in order to negotiate a joint venture with the representative of a small- and-medium-sized Taiwanese company with an international customer- and partner-base. The GLOBE study (House et al., 2004) ranks 61 societal cultures with regard to cultural dimensions (from 1 = highest score to

61 = lowest score for a certain dimension). The wider the gap in ranking, the more notable cross-cultural differences in managerial practices or values are to be expected. For Germany and Taiwan, the GLOBE study suggests the cultural differences set out in Table 2.1.

Table 2.1 German–Taiwanese cultural difference according to GLOBE

Cultural dimension	Societal practice		Societal value	
	Germany	Taiwan	Germany	Taiwan
	Rank	Rank	Rank	Rank
Uncertainty avoidance	5	20	59	8
Power distance	29	32	44	13
Institutional collectivism	54	14	28	15
In-group collectivism	54	20	55	43
Gender egalitarianism	44	42	15	52
Assertiveness	10	42	55	50
Future orientation	13	24	13	46
Performance orientation	22	8	29	36
Humane orientation	61	27	30	46

Note: n = 61, Germany = Germany (West), former FRG

Source: adapted from Mahadevan (2013: 248), based on contributions in House et al. (2004: 248, 250, 251, 304, 306, 362, 365, 366, 409–411, 467–471, 539, 540, 573, 574, 621–623) and Chhokar, Brodbeck and House (2007: 162).

Should the German manager consult this study in advance (which seems sensible), he will be informed that a difference in managerial practice is to be expected, for instance, for assertiveness (higher in Germany) and humane orientation (higher in Taiwan). Still, he should not take this insight as objective fact, for the GLOBE study itself acknowledges the paradoxical nature of culture as both stable and changing. For instance, assertiveness, which seems relevant to German managerial practice, is not highly valued, and we should therefore assume that either the practice is changing or that German managers try to change towards a less assertive style. Conversely, humane orientation seems to be valued less in Taiwan than it is practised.

At this point, the German manager does not yet know the personal details of the representative of the Taiwanese company he is expected to meet. However, based on the GLOBE study's insights that gender egalitarianism is not widely practised and even less valued in Taiwan, he might well expect a male Taiwanese manager.

As these considerations suggest, proceeding from an ethnographic frame of mind does not suggest 'no preparation at all'. Rather, it encourages you to think of yourself as a 'cultural detective' who formulates theory-based hypotheses for your own CCM practice and future cross-cultural scenarios. For instance, in this case, the German manager should be aware that he might be overly assertive when interacting with a Taiwanese manager whom he can expect to be more humane oriented. Still, he should also investigate his own cultural orientation critically, for maybe he implicitly wishes for a less assertive German management and has personally developed a less assertive managerial style.

The ethnographic frame of mind also acknowledges that culture emerges in context, and it unravels relevant cultures and their boundaries from there. In this specific scenario, it is not yet clear as to whether societal cultures are actually the relevant factor influencing the interaction. Both managers have most likely led an international professional life; the German manager himself works for a French multinational company and under a French superior. He will therefore need to pay attention to alternative cultural facets and levels in order to find out which difference is relevant in context.

Being 'prepared' in such an open and ethnographic manner, the German manager now travels to Taiwan. Surprisingly enough, he meets a female Taiwanese manager. At this point, one of the GLOBE study's macro-level hypotheses has been contradicted by micro-level realities. Does this mean that societal norms do not exist? No, it simply means that – despite expecting a gender inequality – the individual female Taiwanese manager has obviously found ways to overcome or navigate around it. This is an important finding, as it is the violation of the cultural norm which sticks in the mind and signals that you might have 'found' a different cultural context and deeper cultural meanings. How should we go about it now? Obviously, the German manager doesn't know much yet, and cannot fully interpret the meaning of this. He will need to ask further questions when experiencing culture in context; you might think of them as refined cultural hypotheses to be tested. With regard to gender egalitarianism, such questions might be: is this a cultural pattern solely in this single company? Are there other female managers, or is she a singular exception? What does it say about corporate culture?

At the same time, the German manager should also relate these considerations back to himself: Germany scores as low on gender egalitarianism as Taiwan on the level of practice, even though the concept seems to be more valued than in Taiwan. So the German manager should ask himself: what are my blind spots when considering female leadership? What are my implicit assumptions of how to see competency? If I am male and used to an assertive managerial style, when and how am I gender-stereotyping (which carries with it the risk of neglecting or undervaluing the competencies of a female manager who originates from a less assertive environment)? This suggests that the ethnographic frame of mind also pays attention to the limitations of the cultural detective's perspective ('the cultural glasses').

On entering the company, the German manager will have the opportunity to observe organizational life and managerial interactions; he can structure culture as 'that complex whole' with the help of the cultural perspective (see Chapter 1), and he can also acknowledge the limitations of his own perspective and his access to the culture of others. He can now ask himself how managers in this company interact, how they '*actually do things around there*', what they have in common, how they differ, and how this relates to himself. From there, the wheel turns again, as these new questions bring about new learning, contradictions and hypotheses in context.

As this example suggests, the ethnographic frame of mind is an *applied* approach for investigating culture in context which is *informed* by ethnography or participant observation as a research method but does not necessarily equal it. Its starting point is cultural curiosity that is directed towards both the seemingly 'normal' and 'everyday' *and* paradoxical exceptions to a previously held assumption. It brings about a circle of cultural investigation, and cultural dimensions are one initial framework for facilitating this process. This framework needs to be tested in context (e.g. Could the other's behaviour be based on a certain understanding of managerial power? Could *I* be influenced by a certain perspective on gender? and so on).

This process enables the cross-cultural manager not only to prepare for cultural norms but also to notice exceptions to them in a specific cultural context. Acting as an 'amateur ethnographer' or 'cultural detective', you can then structure this experience with the help of comparative CCM knowledge. Next, you will need to find out how to make sense of a certain phenomenon in a manner that does culture justice as 'that complex whole' (Tylor, 1871: 1), and for this you need to make culture 'small' and investigate its different facets beyond textbook knowledge and explicit culture, as suggested in Chapter 1.

Again, the facets of culture (Chapter 1) are not clear rules defining CCM, but hypotheses to be tested in action: in some contexts, cultural knowledge might be more important than habitus and practice, in others, material culture might provide the key to understanding others. CCM, at least to my mind, implies that we are aware that culture encompasses all these aspects without defining a priori which of these might influence the specific context wherein we need to act. If one hypothesis should fail, you will simply have to refine previous assumptions and develop and test others. Part of the task is to identify the 'something' that culture is connected to, that is context, and to locate relevant communities of life or meaning.

Ultimately, it is *you* who needs to contextualize cultural dimensions, and their highest value might lie in investigating how our own implicit assumptions could be informed by them. Still, the ethnographic frame of mind, too, is not the formula that will make cultural paradox disappear: culture is and will remain 'puzzling', and it is this realization that should keep you going forward, questioning implicit assumptions and taken-for-granted beliefs, and trying to solve human puzzles. For doing so, the cultural and the comparative cross-cultural perspective complement each other, and an ethnographic frame of mind, common-sense curiosity and a genuine interest in human puzzles are the engine behind this interplay.

Note

1   During World War II, Hall himself had served in the US-American Army abroad, an experience which, I assume, contributed to his later work at the FSI.

3

Intercultural interactions and competence

Being shared, learned and social, culture is essentially a group phenomenon. Still, groups do not interact – individuals interact, and '[t]he extent to which individuals manifest aspects of, or are influenced by, their group or cultural affiliations and characteristics is what makes an interaction an *inter*cultural process' (Spitzberg and Changnon, 2009: 7). This brings about a new perspective to CCM, namely the intercultural interactions approach, which involves both positivist and interpretative viewpoints. In the tradition of Edward T. Hall, this approach investigates culture as communication, albeit a communication that goes beyond words and includes body language, distance, time, context, silence etc. (see Chapter 2). For the time being, we will assume that these 'group/cultural' affiliations loosely correspond to the national/societal cultures we have encountered in Chapter 2, yet it is important to bear in mind that difference in *any* kind of group affiliation might create an *inter*cultural interaction.

Intercultural communication as an applied training discipline emerged in the United States after World War II (Leeds-Hurwitz, 1990; Pusch, 2004; see Chapter 2). As Margaret Pusch observes (2004: 14):

> The intercultural needs that were identified in the United States ... were fairly explicit: Americans had to be prepared to function more effectively and sensitively with strange cultures during overseas assignments; international students, scholars and professionals needed to adapt to the United States as they enrolled and worked in universities and other institutions; and their American hosts needed to relate successfully to and learn from these international sojourners.

Later on, the same skills required for these interactions were also assumed to be essential to US-American diversity 'at home' (Pusch, 2004: 14). This suggests a strong link between intercultural competence 'abroad' and 'elsewhere', and the diversity requirements 'at home' and as concerning our own identities (see Chapter 4).

The discussion of intercultural competence which is part of this chapter is not limited to intercultural communication as a discipline; it originates from a variety of fields, such as communication studies, psychology, applied linguistics and international business and management (see an overview in Spencer-Oatley and Franklin, 2009). Still, I have placed its discussion in the present chapter, due to the strong links between intercultural interactions and intercultural competence. The first link is historic and goes back – among other sources – to the United States Foreign Service Institute (FSI) and Edward T. Hall's need to develop skills for successful interactions abroad (see Chapter 2). Out of this situation, the intercultural training business was born. The second link is implicit to the concepts themselves: without an interactional context to be applied to, intercultural competence cannot manifest itself. This reminds us that intercultural interactions and the competencies required for them go hand in hand, and that both are also linked to a presumed 'mandate to train'.

Key aspects of this chapter are the conceptualizations of intercultural interactions and competence, emics and etics as a key intercultural tool, the differentiation between ritualized and complex interactions, and the need to understand intercultural interactions as negotiated symbolic meaning.

My approach is based on the assumption that any successful CCM practice needs to meet three minimum requirements (which continuously inform each other): becoming aware of the whole of culture (Chapter 1), examining relative difference across cultures and the limitations of our own cultural perspectives (Chapter 2), and moving beyond difference and towards synergies in interpersonal interactions (this chapter). It is here that I introduce the final side to this fundamental 'CCM triangle'.

What will still be missing after this discussion is the question of which cultures are relevant to intercultural interactions (is it only national/societal culture?) and how power discrepancies are an integral part of CCM. These additional (critical) aspects will be the focus points of Chapters 4 and 5 respectively, and they relate back to the cultural, cross-cultural and intercultural perspectives of Chapters 1 to 3 (this just as a preview of the next chapters and as a cautious note that 'intercultural competence' refers to processes of learning and un-learning, rather than a finite and codified outcome).

Emic(s) and etic(s)

Like the cross-cultural approach, the intercultural perspective departs from the dictum of national culture. It does so in a slightly different manner, for it wishes to investigate interactions between representatives of different cultures, based on the assumption that individuals will *perceive* difference in context. This means that macro-level comparisons are applied to a specific micro-contextual purpose, namely to understand what kind of cultural difference matters in context. The focus lies on preparing for *specific* situations, not for the whole of cultural life at home and abroad. To meet this need, only specific patterns of culture and communication are discussed. The models of Edward T. Hall in Chapter 2 exemplify this approach.

A key concept of the intercultural approach is the differentiation between an *emic* (inside) and *etic* (outside) perspective. These terms were coined by US-American linguist Kenneth Pike (Pike, 1967 [1954]; Peterson and Pike, 2002); they originate from the linguistic terms phon*emic* and phon*etic*.

Across disciplines, the terms *emic* and *etic* have come to carry different meanings. In the narrow sense, *emic* and *etic* refer to the understanding that we cannot describe cultural differences objectively, but that we need to assume that culture carries meaning and that this meaning differs across insider–outsider perspectives. This is basically the same differentiation which we have already traced back to interpretivism (Introduction), social constructivism (Chapter 1) and cultural relativism (Chapter 2), as opposed to the idea of a singular cultural reality which is rooted in positivism, objectivism and cultural universalism (e.g. cultural dimensions).

The broader understanding of *emics* and *etics* uses these categories to describe certain approaches to CCM. For instance, you could say that interpretivism is an 'emic' science whereas comparative CCM is an 'etic' science. This differentiation brings about new ways for classifying macro-level CCM – for instance, the Kulturstandard theory (Thomas, Kinast and Schroll-Machl, 2003a, 2003b) mentioned in Chapter 2 can now be understood as an *emic* framework, as opposed to the *etic* framework of cultural dimensions (Spencer-Oatley and Franklin, 2009: 33–34).

Emic and etic as interactional perspectives

The awareness of emic and etic perspectives in the narrow sense reminds us that how you perceive another person's behaviour – or how another person perceives you – tends to be different from the meanings attached to this behaviour from the perspective of those displaying it.

For example, let's say a member of a multicultural team has internalized a culture-specific idea of 'being polite', and another team member has internalized a culture-specific idea of 'being casual'. To simplify matters – as is often done in intercultural training – I will take just these two facets to make up a culture and assume that both individuals are representative of fictitious 'being polite' and 'being casual' cultures. Based on the cultural perspective (see Chapter 1), we can assume that both individuals have culturally learned how to express their respective ideals of 'being polite' and 'being casual' and how to recognize these traits in others. Obviously, like 'real' cultures, these two cultural orientations are not clear-cut rules, but rather a feeling for an acceptable bandwidth of behaviour which meets this ideal.

Now, these two individuals start interacting: what might happen? Well, if they are not aware that they have learned 'different ways of doing things', they might just assume that their respective way of doing things is the only 'normal' way of acting. In this specific interactional context, the polite person might perceive the casual person as rude; the casual person might perceive the polite person as overly stiff. Both views are outside (etic) perspectives, as they judge the other person against their own cultural orientations and are formulated in terms of how the other person's actions do *not* fulfil their own cultural expectations.

Etic perspectives view others mainly as 'what they are not when compared to oneself' – they fail to understand others in their own cultural terms. As a result, perceived negative difference prevails, and mutual learning is obstructed. For instance, in the previous example, the positive emic resources of 'being casual' or 'being polite' become etic shortcomings in the eyes of the respective other, formulated in negative terms of 'this person is not polite enough' or 'this person is not casual enough'.

An awareness of emic and etic in intercultural interactions also informs us that our perceptions of others and our own cultural orientations are interlinked. You might even think of this mechanism the other way round: in order to understand who 'we' are (and why 'our way of doing things' is a good way), we need to construct a category of 'others', namely those 'who we are not' and 'who don't do it the right way'.

For example, we even tend to have 'pictures in mind' of groups of people without having actually met a member of these groups. Are these pictures false or true? Well, as we have them, they are *subjectively* true, even if they are mere stereotypes. So why do we have them if they do not depict objective cultural truths? The purpose of our 'pictures about the other' is to define ourselves (which we can only do via perceiving 'others' as different from 'how we are'). They are etic perceptions and do not portray others in their own terms but only in relation to ourselves. The task might not be to get rid of these 'pictures' (for this may be impossible) but to aim towards self-awareness and moving beyond them when interacting.

We are all limited by our cultural glasses (none of us views the real world), and our perceptions of others serve to define ourselves.

In order to grasp the deeper *meanings* of what seems a strange and alien way of 'doing things', we are required to overcome our own negative (etic) perceptions of others, to change perspective and to interpret the action of others in their own (emic) terms. The trigger point is an unfamiliar or 'strange' situation, and this means that the first step towards intercultural awareness lies in not letting such a situation pass unnoticed (as often happens).

We also need to constantly remind ourselves that 'the way we do things' that feels natural to us is not universal to everyone. It is just 'the way we have come to do things around here and in this specific context'. This makes difference something that is *perceived* in interactions rather than an objective category. To become aware of intercultural situations and our negative perceptions of difference, we need to investigate our interactions: what am I missing here (and how can I become aware), why might another way of doing things be a good way, and what can I learn from it?

Emics and etics as CCM frameworks

The awareness of emics and etics in the broader sense enables us to juggle and combine different CCM perspectives. As US-American communication scholar Bradford J. Hall (2005: 69) notes:

> Compilations of emic observations can help create etic frameworks that in turn can be used to discover and compare emic differences and similarities across cultures. Thus, emic-level findings can help to expand and refine etic knowledge, and etic frameworks can help to discover and enlighten emic concepts.

The complementary use of cultural dimensions as an etic comparative framework and emic-level findings based on an ethnographic frame of mind (see Chapter 2) provides an example. Nonetheless, I prefer the more narrow usage of the terms emic and etic, namely as referring to the inside and outside perspective in interactions. The rationale behind it is that the comparative cross-cultural perspective does not acknowledge that there might be any other reality than the positivist, objective and culturally-universalist one. It is only from an interpretative, social constructivist and culturally-relative perspective that you can identify cultural dimensions as an 'etic' framework: to understand 'etics', you also need the awareness that such a thing as 'emics' exists in the first place. If you lack the latter, then 'etics' become the only reality available to you.

Still, the broader understanding of emics and etics in CCM can be useful for figuring out which perspective to apply to which aspect of culture. For instance, sociologists Thomas Berger and Peter Luckmann (1966), two founders of social constructivism, differentiate between *objective* culture and *subjective* culture. The first refers to societal frameworks, structures and institutions. The second refers to the *meaning* given to these frameworks and other aspects of life by those in social interaction. Whereas objective culture can be assumed to be 'just there' (a legal system of a country simply exists), the latter involves emic and etic perspectives (how a legal system is perceived). This suggests that objective culture might be more suitable to objectivist theoretical frameworks, e.g. cultural dimensions (etics) than subjective culture which might be best studied via interpretative approaches, e.g. participant observation (emics), and vice versa.

We are therefore asked not to confuse objective and subjective culture. For instance, the cultural perceptions linked to subjective culture tend to be more internally heterogeneous than unifying objective cultural frameworks (not every national 'insider' interprets the legal system of their country in the same way, yet they are subject to the same laws). Cultural perceptions are also more likely to change than objective cultural frameworks (depending on how your life evolves, a certain aspect of the law might seem more or less just than it used to seem). This reminds us that, when managing across cultures or trying to gather cultural information, we should carefully examine which aspect of culture a certain source of information deals with, whether it does so from an emic or etic perspective, and whether its underlying theoretical framework (emics or etics) fits the aspect of culture it concerns.

Conceptualizations of intercultural competence

Let's say you wish to perform well in a multicultural team or as an international leader in a multinational company. Wouldn't it be reassuring if you could inform yourself of the requirements of 'how to do things interculturally' or train yourself accordingly?

Unfortunately, intercultural competence is by no means a unified concept, and the term 'competence' itself is highly debated (Deardorff, 2006).[1] What seems agreed upon is that competence shows via performance in a certain situation, that it can be somewhat (but not fully) developed, and that it distinguishes high-performing individuals from low-performing individuals. The tricky thing, of course, is to come up with a definition of all these variables (what is meant by performance?)

and with ways of assessing them (how to measure one performance against the other?).

Intercultural competence is also not the only term which has been used in the literature. Over the course of time, scholars from various disciplines have spoken, for instance, of 'intercultural sensitivity' (J.M. Bennett and M.J. Bennett, 2004), 'intercultural interaction competence' (Spencer-Oatley and Franklin, 2009), 'intercultural communication competence' (Chen and Starosta, 2005), 'intercultural competence' (Deardorff, 2009; Spitzberg and Changnon, 2009), or – in international management – 'a global mindset' (Kedia and Mukherji, 1999). To simplify matters, I will use 'intercultural competence' as the umbrella term for all the different terminologies that have been put forward. Later in this chapter, we will also come across the term 'cultural intelligence' (Earley and Ang, 2003), which has emerged as an alternative concept.

In their historic overview of the development of concepts of intercultural competence, US-American communication scholars Brian Spitzberg and Gabrielle Changnon (2009) identify the need for corporate, organizational or competitive national success as the underlying motivation for becoming and making others interculturally competent (the same can be said for the individual herself/himself who wishes to compete in the global marketplace). In the 1960s and 1970s, this need led to a search for the components of intercultural competence, and the coining of terms such as *intercultural competence* or *intercultural effectiveness* (Spitzberg and Changnon, 2009: 9).

This reminds us that intercultural competence is linked to a desired outcome. Brian Spitzberg (2000: 379–380), for instance, defines the successful application of intercultural competence as the ability to interact effectively and appropriately with members of other cultures and/or to influence an intercultural interactional context in an effective and appropriate manner. Effectiveness refers to the ability to reach their goals; appropriateness requires not losing sight of the other person's interests when doing so. Intercultural competence is also related to our own communicative goals. For instance, US-American intercultural communication scholars Guo-Ming Chen and William Starosta (2005: 241) speak of intercultural communication competence as 'the ability to effectively and appropriately execute communication behaviors to elicit a desired response in a specific environment'.

Intercultural competence is also related to a certain context. Most theories proceed from the individual while also acknowledging the importance of other contextual factors. US-American political scientist Jane Bennett and intercultural communication scholar Milton

Bennett (2004: 149), for instance, conceive intercultural competence as 'the ability to communicate effectively in cross-cultural situations and to relate appropriately in a variety of cultural contexts'.

Most theories agree that intercultural competence involves a complex set of abilities and/or dispositions that link knowledge and practice. Often-stated components are affective (emotional), behavioural (conative) and cognitive elements (Gudykunst, Wiseman and Hammer, 1977), or, in a later theory (Spitzberg, 2000), motivation (involving emotion and affection), knowledge (rooted in cognitive processes) and skills (related to behaviour and action).

Most conceptualizations view intercultural competence as requiring intercultural *experience*. They differ regarding whether certain individuals have a higher disposition towards intercultural competence or whether and how this ability can and should be trained or learned.

Whereas some theories wish to identify the components of intercultural competence (what intercultural competence *is*), others investigate how to *become* interculturally competent. Based on this differentiation, I will focus on *intercultural competence as a process* (e.g. of development, learning or adaptation) and *intercultural competence as a composition* (e.g. of contributing factors, elements of comprehension or patterns of cause-and-effect).[2] I will also discuss *cultural intelligence* as an alternative concept.

Intercultural competence as a process

Process-oriented models of intercultural competence focus on how to become interculturally competent. Many models have assumed that individuals move from *ethnocentric* to *ethnorelative* stages (e.g. M.J. Bennett, 1986) when experiencing differences. At first, another culture is measured against a person's own culture (which can be considered an insufficient – you might say etic – perception of others), next, it is viewed in its own (emic) terms. This suggests that interculturally competent – or you might also say culturally-aware – individuals experience the social world in a more complex and multifaceted way than less interculturally competent/culturally-aware individuals. Differentiating this process further, Milton Bennett (1986) proposes three ethnocentric stages of experiencing difference, namely *denial* ('my cultural perspective is the only one that exists'), *defence* ('my culture is better than theirs' or, if reversed by a process of 'over-adaptation', 'their culture is better than mine') and *minimization* ('their culture is different, but it's actually only a (lesser) variant of my culture', for instance, when a European manager assumes that the situation at the low-cost offshore production site mirrors the stage of industrialization in 19th-century Europe). All these stages are considered insufficient. After having overcome the last ethnocentric stage of *minimization*, individuals might move through three ethnorelative stages of experiencing difference. First, difference is *accepted* ('cultural differences truly exist', for instance, when accepting that there is no universal or natural style of 'good leadership'), next, there is *adaptation* ('maybe I will change my ways of doing things to be more like their way of doing things', for instance, when trying out aspects of another leadership style), and finally, *integration* ('I want to combine their and my way', for instance, when intergrating different aspects into an intercultural leadership style).

It is also assumed that individuals move through different phases of *culture shock* when experiencing intercultural difference and the related need for *adjustment*. These phases are often depicted as a U-curve (Oberg, 1960) or double U-curve (J.R. Gullahorn and J.E. Gullahorn, 1962). In its most simple variation, the U-curve suggests that, at first, individuals are highly satisfied or motivated when interacting interculturally (the *'honeymoon phase'* – 'this is a great experience, and I can do this!'). Next, satisfaction drops and individuals experience *culture shock and crisis* ('this is harder than I thought, and I quit!'), and sometimes even become hostile towards the other culture and withdraw from it. If individuals manage *recovery* – for instance, via humour and ambivalence – and dare to re-enter the alien cultural environment ('I can still do it, and will try to do so again!'), their adjustment satisfaction rises again to moderate levels. Finally, they might reach *adjustment* on a high level of satisfaction which is slightly lower than the initial euphoric 'honeymoon' level.

Implicit to process-oriented models is the understanding that an individual *moves* to another culture – for instance, an expatriate, a sojourner or a migrant – and then needs to successfully face questions of *adjustment* (overcome culture shock), *assimilation* (blend in or become similar to the host culture) and *adaptation* (change their ways of doing things in microcultural interactions and make adjustments to the macro-cultural environment). We could therefore say that these models are applicable to 'classic' CCM scenarios – for instance, negotiations, first contact or business meetings. These are often characterized by easily definable cultural difference ('them' versus 'us') and often involve actual physical movement. They might be less suitable to complex interactions – such as global and dispersed teams, virtual project-work, or intercultural leadership in a multinational company – wherein multiple and overlapping categories of difference interact in multiple contexts. For these contexts, it may be more helpful to understand intercultural competence as a composition, and we will do so in the following.

Intercultural competence as a composition

Another type of model tries to identify certain components of intercultural competence (*compositional models*) or the factors which facilitate comprehension in intercultural interactions (*co-orientational models*). Some of them are static whereas others look at the cause-and-effect of different components or factors, or a combination thereof.

Generally speaking, intercultural competence is assumed to emerge from a combination of *attitudes* (e.g. openness, curiosity, devaluing ethnocentrism and discrimination), *knowledge* (e.g. of one's own cultural identity, cultural differences and similarities), and *skills* (e.g. one's ability to engage in self-reflection, take multiple perspectives or understand differences in multiple contexts). These are linked to an individual's *motivation* (e.g. the wish to enrich one's life via cross-cultural experiences). As a specific example, British language scholar Michael Byram's (1997) model has become particularly relevant in foreign language teaching with its additional goal to facilitate intercultural competence. Byron proposes that intercultural competence not only comprises *knowledge, attitudes, critical cultural awareness, interaction and discovery skills*, and *interpreting and relating skills*, but is also intertwined with various levels of linguistic competence. This approach exemplifies the strong ties between culture (as understood from an intercultural communication perspective) and language.

The problem is that culture is more than language and often tacit (see Chapter 1), and that some concepts, such as 'clear communication' or 'openness', do not have a singular and direct behavioural expression; we can only deduce them from other acts and as related to our own cultural experiences. This reminds us that intercultural competence manifests in many ways, and that each and every one of us needs to develop our own management style in the best possible way.

US-American scholar Darla Deardorff (2006) acknowledges this dilemma and assumes that the visible desired external outcomes of intercultural competence – such as behaving and communicating effectively and appropriately based on intercultural skills, knowledge and behaviour and achieving our own goals – are informed by a desired internal outcome by which an individual filters experience (e.g. the degree of adaptability, empathy or flexibility, or the ability to take an ethnorelative viewpoint). The desired internal outcome, which is grounded in motivation, skills and knowledge, guides individual behaviour in context, and is in return informed by further experiences. This constitutes a process that relates individuals and their interactions with others in context

In summary, culture as a composition informs us that many aspects need to come together for something like 'intercultural competence' to

show. This perspective is helpful for reaching and maintaining awareness with regard to what is involved, still, it cannot tell us how to
actually 'be' interculturally competent or whether this involves trained
abilities or given dispositions.

Cultural intelligence as an alternative concept

Competence becomes visible in context, and the individual is not the
only factor influencing context. In the literature on intercultural competence, it has therefore been heavily debated as to whether it's possible
to identify universal components of intercultural competence which are
applicable to *all* contexts. In this process, the concept of *cultural intelligence* emerged (Earley and Ang, 2003).

Cultural intelligence, also referred to as 'cultural quotient (CQ)',
describes 'a person's capability to adapt effectively to new cultural contexts' (Earley and Ang, 2003: 59). This capability is assumed to have a
combined cognitive, motivational and behavioural basis, and '[w]ithout
all these facets acting in concert, a person does not display cultural
intelligence' (Earley and Ang, 2003: 59).

The concept of cultural intelligence aims at integrating individual,
motivational and contextual/environmental factors that contribute to
intelligence (as manifesting itself in new cultural contexts). It also tries to
integrate context-specific and universal conceptualizations of intercultural competence. On the one hand, it accounts for general factors of
intelligence (linguistic, logical-mathematical and spatial) which are
assumed to be culturally universal. One the other hand, it assumes that
intelligence is more than functioning in academic tests, but requires a
social setting. Or, as P. Christopher Earley and Soon Ang (2003: 58) state:

> ... we see cultural intelligence as a concept that spans internal and
> external views such that cultural intelligence is not determined by
> a person's intelligent cognition, motivation, and behaviour alone,
> but also includes a person's mental intellect and behaviors as it
> relates to his or her functioning and adaptation in new or multiple
> cultural environments.

This terminology reminds us that even concepts such as 'intelligence'
might be relational, that is, not rooted in the individual but in her/his
relations to others in a specific context, and this might be the major
contribution of this wording, as related to other studies on intelligence.
Still, cultural intelligence – as the presumably less 'fuzzy' version of

intercultural competence – might be utilized by companies and consul-
tancies to assess the 'CQ' of present and future human resources. If the
concept is exploited in such a way, we might observe the same shortcomings as with the misuse of quantifiable cultural dimensions as
business etiquette prescriptions(see Chapter 2).

A focus on the symbolic meanings of ritualized interactions

Competence manifests itself in context, and the previous sections have
provided insights into this link. At the FSI, Edward T. Hall had a specific
context in mind for which to develop intercultural competencies,
namely foreign service personnel to be sent abroad for diplomatic, and
sometimes military, missions. This context, like 'traditional' CCM,
which is characterized by the actual physical movement of individuals
(for example, so-called expatriates being sent abroad), involves a large
portion of ritualized interactions, such as negotiations, formal meetings,
first contact scenarios, visiting delegations etc.

Rituals are social events of high importance which are characterized
by a high degree of homogeneity (Turner, 1977). They simplify otherwise 'complex' social interactions, and the differentiation between
ritualized and complex interactions (such as multicultural teams or
virtual project work in a multinational company) is important to bear
in mind.

Rituals can either fail or succeed, based on whether a successful social
transition is made or not. This transition is socially important but is
expressed by seemingly 'simple' things which are usually ritually prescribed without much variation. For instance, during a wedding
ceremony, there are clear rules on how the individuals involved shall
make it clear that they wish to proceed from an 'unmarried' to a
'married' state, and because of the high social importance of this step
there is not much variation in how to express this crucial meaning.

When interacting ritually, managers do seemingly 'simple' things,
e.g. shake hands, bow, offer tea or coffee, engage in certain culturally-
learned versions of small-talk (or not), and so on. Their purpose lies not
with these small social acts as such; rather, these acts are symbolically
significant for a wider transition to be made. Those offering drinks, making comments on the weather etc. do not *really* (or merely) wish to take
refreshments or inquire about the latest weather report. Rather, they
want to signal crucial meanings for the intended managerial or corporate corporation, such as 'good relations', 'competence', 'motivation to

cooperate', etc., thereby facilitating the transition towards this very goal. Often, it is at this point that the cultural differences in management and business show (Mahadevan, 2015b).

The *real* conflict, though, is not that some party has offered tea and biscuits at the beginning of a negotiation and that the other party finds this a waste of time and wishes to present their technological prototype instead. Rather, both parties wish to express symbolic meanings. For doing so, they have learned culture-specific and ritualized ways of showing commitment, competency, motivation, excellence, leadership, and so on. The actual problem is that they cannot put their message across and also receive confusing messages from the other side.

This suggests that we need to pay particular attention to 'simple' and 'small' phenomena and acts in ritualized interactions in order to uncover their underlying cultural patterns and wider meanings, for instance, from an ethnographic frame of mind. The following section presents an example of such an approach.

The case of English weather-speak

British Anthropologist Kate Fox (2004: 25) observes that when *Watching the English* (this is the title of her book), '[A]ny English conversation, must begin with The Weather.' You could now say, but what is the difference between this – presumably – ethnographic focus on 'simple things' and the business etiquette approach, which has been discarded as insufficient in Chapter 2? The difference is that Kate Fox has inferred the importance of 'The Weather' from an ethnographic investigation of culture as 'that complex whole' which enabled her to identify patterns in conversations about 'The Weather' and to view these as *ritualized* and *symbolic* behaviour. Fox states (2004: 26):

> ... our conversations about the weather are not really about the weather at all: English weather-speak is a form of code, evolved to help us overcome our natural reserve ... [Statements about the weather] are not requests for meteorological data: they are ritual greetings, conversation-starters or default 'fillers'.

This statement points to the deep symbolic meanings of a simple ritual. It also reminds us that rituals serve a purpose: they wish to make complex culture simple and they propose clear interaction patterns for doing so.

Kate Fox (2004: 26–36) has identified the following 'rules of English weather-speak'. First, there is the requirement of *reciprocity* – if one person speaks about the weather, the other needs to do so as well. There is the need to agree upon the weather ('openers such as "Cold, isn't it?" must be reciprocated'; Fox, 2004: 28), and of a shared understanding of the exceptions to the *agreement rule*. There also is a weather *hierarchy rule* (a socially-agreed upon rating of weather expressions from best to worse). 'Sunny and warm/mild', for example, is the best ritualized weather option, whereas 'rainy and cool/cold' is the worst (Fox, 2004: 31). This enables speakers to reciprocate a weather-related statement, except regarding the worst weather (rainy and cool/cold), with a ritualized 'But at least it's not ...' introduction to the next worst weather scenario (Fox, 2004: 31). Snow, being 'aesthetically pleasing, but practically inconvenient', is subject to a *moderation rule* requiring that 'too much snow, like too much of anything, is to be deplored' (Fox, 2004: 32). Fox also states that whereas the English are allowed, and even socially obliged, to critique the weather, foreigners should not do so. She also identifies listening to and exchanging the content of the Shipping Forecast as key ritualistic activity related to the social dimensions of 'The Weather'.

The CCM implications of 'simple things'

As Kate Fox's (2004) ethnographic analysis suggests, there is much more to English weather-speak than just asking questions about the weather, and outsiders are prone to 'getting it wrong'. For those familiar with it, this complex procedure will be just a 'simple thing', so they might not even be aware of how it contributes to a social interaction but only notice their uneasiness or perceive another person as annoying if their expectations are not met.

To the outsider or learner of culture, identifying these patterns and dealing with the surprise, puzzlement and confusion which arises from seemingly 'strange' behaviour, the purpose of which remains unclear, is a key part of what you might call intercultural competence or the ability to 'learn' another culture.[3]

Negotiations, first-contact scenarios or business meetings are the classic examples of ritualized interactions in CCM. For example, 'weather-speak' might be an established opener to an intra-cultural (English) negotiation, meeting or first-contact situation, but could result in failure across or between cultures.

When experiencing conflict, individuals might also fall back on ritualized behaviour in complex interactions. For example, multicultural teams need to find new shared meaning, behaviour styles, interpretations etc. while working together (Mahadevan, 2015b), and this requires complex and non-ritualized interactions which can hardly be prescribed. Still, in times of conflict, individuals might 'fall back' on those culture-specific ways which they have learned are established ritualized 'conflict-solvers'. They might, for instance, apply a certain laconic 'English humour' to a disastrous event (Fox, 2004) or analyse and verbalize the problem with 'German meticulousness' (Schroll-Machl, 2003). The respective option chosen is not a strategic managerial decision, but the unconscious implementation of a socially-learned pattern for symbolically minimizing a conflict via a ritualized behaviour that has seemed adequate and appropriate in the past.

What does a focus on the symbolic meaning of ritualized interactions mean for our CCM practice? First, it reminds us that 'what people do must make sense to them, otherwise they would not do it'. This sense might not be explicit – no one learns English 'weather-speak' in the same way they would learn facts from a textbook. Rather, individuals grow into it as a 'normal way of doing things' that carries symbolic meaning. We should therefore try to find symbolic meaning in these presumably 'simple things', while at the same time bearing in mind that ritualized interactions do not cover every aspect of CCM.

The intercultural interactionist approach assumes that macro-cultural difference manifests itself in micro-individual interactions. When applying this perspective, we should be aware that most scenarios cover situations which we might now understand as ritualized. This suggests that conceptualizations of intercultural communication or competence may not be suitable for complex interactions and that differences originating from macro-cultural concepts such as cultural dimensions (Chapter 2) might only manifest themselves in ritualized behaviour. To find new, intercultural 'ways of doing things', we therefore need to consider the contexts for which an intercultural management recommendation was and is intended, to be aware that the tools of the intercultural approach mainly suit ritualized interactions, and to investigate those situations wherein we ourselves fall back on ritualized behaviour.

Conclusion: negotiating meaning in intercultural interactions

This chapter has shed light on key aspects of the intercultural interactions perspective, such as emic(s) and etic(s), and intercultural competence and intelligence. It has added to this perspective by discussing the need to investigate the symbolic meanings of ritualized interactions, and to differentiate between objective and subjective culture. It proposed that macro-level differences are most likely to show in ritualized micro-level interactions, but that complex interactions might require alternative tools.

The concept of intercultural competence remains highly debated. It is, for example, uncertain whether intercultural competence is acquired or a 'given' personal trait, or whether it is culture-relative or universal. Likewise, when investigating how individuals, culture and context are related, one might either assume that the desired outcome of intercultural interactions lies in adaptation to a certain culture, or that the desired outcome is a 'normality or familiarity with differences' (Rathje, 2007). The first viewpoint assumed that 'culture unifies' individuals, the second proposed that culture 'glues' remaining differences together as a new and culture-specific intercultural sphere. Together, both metaphors might be linked to the paradox of culture, namely the insight that it is both regular and variable (see an overview in Spencer-Oatley and Franklin, 2009: 36–38). To account for both aspects, CCM scholars Laurence Romani, Sonja Sackmann and Henriett Primecz (2011) have therefore proposed speaking of 'negotiated meaning' instead of 'symbolic meaning'.

Understanding intercultural interactions as negotiated meanings acknowledges that they include both the perseverance of cultural regularity *and* the creation of new intercultural variability. For instance, Pierre Bourdieu's concept of habitus (1986) proposes that practice is based on collective regularities of 'how to behave', yet it also differs from it (humans are both the producers and products of culture). In the words of Helen Spencer-Oatley and Peter Franklin (2009: 36), 'people incorporate into their habitus the regularities they experience over time both in and across given contexts, yet their actual practice emerges from a dynamic interaction of these regularities with improvisation and creativity'. Likewise, an English counterpart in negotiations might behave in line with 'weather-speak' regularities, or improvise creatively, or use a combination of these strategies based on multiple factors. These factors also include an individual's expectation that a member of another culture *will* indeed be different, which already changes how individuals behave and interpret others. Secondly, our motivations to deal with and overcome difference play a crucial role. This reminds us that we cannot prescribe either the outcome or the content of intercultural interactions. Intercultural competence therefore also involves the ability to hold multiple hypotheses in mind when interacting and negotiating meaning.

Notes

1   If you wish to read more about intercultural competence, I recommend *The Sage Handbook of Intercultural Competence*, edited by Darla Deardorff (2009), particularly the discussion of intercultural competence by Brian Spitzberg and Gabrielle Changnon (2009). Helen Spencer-Oatley and Peter Franklin (2009) also provide a good overview of the discussion, as do Dan Landis, Janet Bennett and Milton Bennett (2004) and Guo-Ming Chen and William Starosta (2005). All these books are interdisciplinary – still, the angle from which they approach the subject differs slightly and in complementary ways. Deardorff's work originates from higher education, Spencer-Oatley and Franklin are rooted in applied linguistics. Landis, Bennett and Bennett (2004) are more oriented towards social psychology, whereas Chen and Starosta (2005) lean slightly towards anthropological/sociological concepts.

2   My selection is based on Spitzberg and Changnon (2009). In their excellent overview of the literature, the authors categorize contemporary models into *compositional models* (what are the components of intercultural competence?), *co-orientational models* (how is comprehension – understood as involving understanding, overlapping perspectives, accuracy, directness, and clarity – reached?), *developmental models* (how does competence – either individually or in relation to others, or as a combination thereof – evolve?), *adaptational models* (how does the process of adaptation – understood as a criterion of competence – evolve?), and *causal path models* (which measurable paths of cause and effect lead to intercultural competence?). The authors conclude their overview with an extensive list of components associated with interpersonal, communicative and intercultural competence, which is clustered into *motivation, knowledge, higher-order skills* (how to use a certain ability), *macro-level skills and competencies,* (micro-level) *skills* – further differentiated into *attentiveness, composure, coordination* and *expressiveness – contextual competencies, outcomes* and *context.* For the purposes of this book, I have simplified this overview.

3   If you wish to read more about how culture can be identified in the 'everyday', I suggest reading the whole of *Watching the English* (Fox, 2004), not in order to learn about 'how the English are' (which you will, too), but so as to immerse yourself into an example of what an ethnographic approach to culture might look like, what it pays attention to, and what you might learn from it for CCM.

4

Diversity and identity

The previous chapters introduced the cultural, the comparative cross-cultural and the intercultural interactionist perspective as three complementary sides of the CCM triangle. The rationale behind this approach was the assumption that any successful CCM practice needs to meet three minimum requirements (which inform each other): becoming aware of what culture involves (Chapter 1), examining relative differences and similarities across cultures and the limitations of one's own cultural perspective (Chapter 2), and moving beyond perceptions of difference and towards synergies in interpersonal interactions (Chapter 3). The latter involves individual knowledge, skills, behaviour and motivation, as well as reflexive interactions, and the investigation and experience of culture in context. The concept of intercultural competence (Chapter 3) proposes that it enables individuals to 'see more' when interacting (as does the idea of an ethnographic frame of mind); it is yet another tool for the cultural detective.

Solving cultural puzzles also involves questioning previously held beliefs or holding multiple perspectives in mind, either simultaneously or one after the other. To this end, the present chapter challenges the assumption that national and societal cultural differences are the ones that matter for CCM. It investigates diversity and alternative collective identities ('who we are in relation to others'), within and beyond perceived cultural borders, and as related to power effects.

The key themes of this chapter are multiple cultures and alternative group-related identifications (such as professional and organizational cultures, or social class), critical diversity markers (such as race, ethnicity, gender, age, etc.), majority–minority relations, and identity beyond presumed cultural borders (e.g. hybrid or bicultural identities). Most concepts originate from sociology, anthropology and diversity studies and are not normally part of a CCM text (but should be, due to reasons which will be discussed). To develop these concepts into a critical CCM tool, I have combined them with the postmodern technique of 'deconstruction' (Derrida, 1978) to form what I would like to call the 'critical multiple cultures perspective'.

Acknowledging this perspective might enable us to overcome three implicit dangers of CCM theory and practice, namely overstating the importance of national/societal cultural differences, exaggerating (macro-) cultural homogeneity and regularity, and assuming that intercultural interactions are power-free. All issues manifest themselves in the intercultural training business, which is the reason why my argument departs from this context. This example also provides a link to the previous chapter.

Insights from the intercultural training business

Intercultural training refers to a preparatory, often group-focused course of about one to two days on a specific topic. Courses can be broadly differentiated into 'doing business in [a specific country]' and general 'cultural awareness/intercultural communication'. Their purpose, or at least their unique selling proposition, is to 'make' individuals interculturally competent, either in general or as related to a specific business culture or CCM task.

Intercultural training promotes methods such as role play, so-called critical incidents (specific situations and misunderstandings from which wider cultural learning can be derived, e.g. Thomas, Kinast and Schroll-Machl, 2003a, 2003b), case studies and simulations over or in addition to a facts-oriented transmission of knowledge and language training (Pusch, 2004: 15). The underlying assumption is that interactional and experiential learning – learning that involves behaviour and emotions beyond cognition – might be the closest one can come to actual intercultural experience. Implicit to the idea of simulating actual experience with other methods is the understanding that the recipients of intercultural training lack prior intercultural experiences. Following this understanding, the focus of intercultural training often lies on *preparing* for another culture.

Intercultural training is also a 'hands-on' field: its practical concepts and methods for cultural preparation 'emerged from experience and [were] built on practical application', rather than 'from abstract intellectual inquiry' (Pusch, 2004: 15). Training material often speaks of culture in terms of metaphors, such as 'culture as an onion' (Geert Hofstede), 'culture as an iceberg' (Edward T. Hall), or 'we relate to culture like fish to the water' (Fons Trompenaars and Hampden-Turner). This can be considered an attempt to make culture as intuitive and comprehensible as possible for those trained.

Corporate intercultural training activities, particularly those in multinational corporations, take place in an 'intercultural training triangle' which involves three distinct groups (Mahadevan and Mayer, 2012).

These are those to be trained; the corporate Human Resource (HR) department commissioning, selecting and evaluating specific trainers and training activities; and external intercultural trainers, the 'Interculturalists' (Dahlén, 1997). In their interactions, we can observe how market pressures encourage the belief in national cultural differences and their negative consequences, and a focus on standardized intercultural training tools. This example also allows us to identify multiple cultures and to understand how perceptions of difference are related to divergent identity-related interests and motivations.

The need to buy and sell standardized cross-national cultural differences

Intercultural training is not a formalized professional field, despite trainers in many countries being loosely connected to SIETAR (the Society for Intercultural Education, Training and Research). Due to this lack of formal requirements, HR managers (who might not be well versed in intercultural theory themselves) face a 'buying problem': who shall they choose to deliver an intercultural training, what are the criteria for selection, and how can they evaluate the success of an intercultural training activity?

Market pressures play a role, and the more you can pack into one or two days of training, the better it might seem. When working as an intercultural trainer, I heard HR managers say things such as 'we only have one day, there are 25 people to be trained, and we need cultural awareness and how to do business in India, China, Russia and the Middle East', accompanied by a 'yes, we know, this is not ideal, but this is the only thing we could get HR money for … '.

This reminds us that intercultural training is a *business* with market pressures and the 'need to sell' or 'buy' national cultural difference. It might say less about what intercultural trainers and HR managers *really* wish to train – or whether they even prefer intercultural training over other methods[1] – and more about what the external and internal market, as structured via the intercultural training triangle, deems to be cost-efficient and cost-effective.

As a result, interculturalists (who need a job, after all) need to make the impossible possible, and this inevitably leads to standardized comparative tools, such a cultural dimensions or Kulturstandards (culture standards; see Chapter 2). According to Swedish anthropologist Tommy Dahlén (1997), the bestselling strategy might be the one that stresses the existence and negative impact of national cultural differences ('country xyz is *so* different that your project will fail without an intercultural training session'). This way, the interculturalist affirms her/his position as the (only) expert to overcome national cultural difference ('but *I* know exactly what your employees need').

To simplify selection, and to standardize training execution and evaluation, HR managers, particularly those in larger companies, might also choose intercultural training agencies (who represent numerous trainers) over individual freelance interculturalists (who are often 'country experts'). This again strengthens the need for a measurable and standardized content across all the training activities provided by an intercultural training agency.

HR also has to convince corporate leaders, the internal cost-accounting department, and sometimes those to be trained, that their investment in intercultural training is justified. This means that HR, too, has to sell 'negative cross-national cultural differences' internally to support their claim. In order to do so, HR managers (who are not the intercultural experts themselves) might rely on the interculturalists' input, which is passed on to those making corporate decisions on intercultural training activities. All these aspects further affirm the need to 'buy' or 'sell' standardized, negative, cross-national cultural differences.

Multiple cultures and identity-related perceptions of negative difference

Often those to be trained are not the ones making the decision about who is going to train them and how, as this is the intermediate HR department's expertise. At this point, multiple cultures and perceptions of negative difference intersect.

For example, in the case of engineers or engineering-management to be trained, HR often assumes these professions are 'less socially competent' than management. In the words of an HR manager (Mahadevan, 2011a: 92, 95): '[Engineers] simply don't have enough social skills ... You can't even have a structured meeting with these people [the engineers]! How are we supposed to teach them advanced intercultural competency!'

So is this negative perception an objective fact or an etic perspective which fails to grasp emic meanings? Engineering is a social activity after all, so there *must* be an 'engineering way' of expressing and recognizing 'social skills'.

It might also be that the engineering department to be interculturally trained rejects the need for such a training based on the firm belief that national cultural differences do not exist or at least do not play a role in global engineering (Mahadevan, 2011a, 2012a). So how should HR or an external interculturalist react to this statement? Both might take it as proof of a lack of intercultural competence. This interpretation might even contribute positively to HR managers' or the intercultualists' self-image: their perceived usefulness, their image of self, and their corporate legitimacy might depend on it. This reminds us that HR managers and interculturalists have a *need* and a *motivation* for national cultural differences to exist and to trump the alternative (emic) belief in global engineering which is specific to an engineering professional culture.

Still, the emic perspective of a global engineering community also seems plausible: the fundamentals of science are independent of culture (concepts such as gravity are not culture-specific, and Newton's apple falls down in every culture). Managing technology might indeed be less culturally-relative (in the comparative cross-cultural sense) than managing people. Engineers are also united by theories, practices and methods that are unique to their community of practice (see Chapter 1), and when interacting interculturally in specific contexts they rely on specialized knowledge which outsiders, such as HR management or intercultural trainers, do not possess. So how can we be sure that national cultural difference outweighs all other 'ways of doing things'? If intercultural competence is at least partly context-related (as we must assume), then it might well be that HR managers and interculturalists do *not* know what kind of intercultural competencies are required in engineering (Mahadevan and Mayer, 2012). So are national cultural differences *really* the most relevant to this context? Maybe engineering and managerial cultures are the most relevant categories to be considered? Maybe the interculturalists as organizational outsiders are the cultural aliens?

On the other hand, engineers, too, might pursue their own identity- and status-related interests and *make* certain engineers different if it suits their purposes. For instance, I have also experienced that some established headquarter engineers perceived new (and less labour-cost intensive) offshore site engineers as less competent in order to defend themselves from being laid off (Mahadevan, 2011a). Those afraid of losing their jobs found proof for this perspective, which they communicated to higher management, in the intercultural training selected by HR and provided by an intercultural trainer (for instance, the presumed polychronic nature of an Indian working style was presented as proof of why Indian engineers were unable to meet schedule requirements). Those who felt secure perceived Indian engineers as 'engineers, too', who were no different from any other member of a global community of practice. This suggests that perceptions of difference are also related to people's own identity fears. At the same time, national cultural differences *do* exist – but what is their impact on the individual in context?

So which belief should HRM and intercultural trainers affirm in such a situation – global engineering or national cultural differences?

Majority–minority relations play their role as well. In the previously discussed company, all but one of the engineering managers (and most engineers) were male, and in the internal 'downsizing war' female offshore engineers were often worse off than male offshore engineers, as the male majority across both sites tended to unconsciously devalue female competencies to secure their own jobs. At the same time, females at the headquarters were often better off than those at the offshore site (Mahadevan, 2015a).

This suggests that the intercultural training triangle – presumably like many or most CCM contexts – is also an arena for power and identity struggles. These mechanisms are linked to conflicting identity needs and motivations, to majority–minority relations, and to the general pressures of a profit-oriented environment.

Multiple cultures and collective identities

The previous example highlights the interplay between multiple cultures, such as national, organizational, departmental, professional, site cultures, and many more. When I speak of a 'multiple cultures perspective' in this book, I refer to an approach that acknowledges the possibility that *any* of these cultures might be the most relevant marker of difference in a complex context (not only national or societal culture).

CCM scholars take different positions in this debate. Some (e.g. McSweeney, 2009) focus on how nations are internally heterogeneous and culturally diverse; they critique the sole focus on national cultures. Others find political national cultures (Chevrier, 2009; d'Iribarne, 2009) or national cultural values (Minkov and Hofstede, 2012) to be fairly homogeneous, even in global management, or in multi-ethnic and multi-lingual nations.

A critical CCM requires us to juggle and combine both assumptions when studying or experiencing cultural differences. For example, we might need to interpret organizational cultures independent of nationality (Witte, 2012), while still entertaining the possibility of dominant cross-national differences, for instance, as related to corporate values (d'Iribarne, 2012) or managerial learning styles (Barmeyer, 2004). It is via this paradox that our sense of 'who we are in relation to others' – our identities – emerges.

Identity describes a concept of self which seems 'fixed' but changes over time (e.g. Weedon, 2004; Lawler, 2008; Jackson II and Hogg, 2010).

It requires both identification and recognition (S. Hall, 1990), both of which are ongoing, interlinked processes of relating oneself to others. For instance, when considering what it takes to be 'British', individuals not only relate to familiar ideas about national belonging, they also recognize others as belonging within this category or not (S. Hall, 1990).

Identity is defined in relation to others, particularly in relation to 'who one is not' (Weedon, 2004: 19). It emerges as a two-way process, namely via ascriptions made by others ('who others think you are') and processes of self-referencing ('who you yourself think you are'). Researchers therefore speak of 'social identity' (Lawler, 2008) or 'collective identity' (Baumann, 1996). This implies that humans do not *have* an identity in the sense of a self-sufficient, autonomous self or a process which occurs solely *within* the individual, but that we all *learn* identity through others. For example, we are familiar with our specific national identities and the requirements of how to express them.

We could even assume that collective identities (understood as 'who I am in relation to others') and culture are one and the same, and you might try this hypothesis out by substituting 'culture' with 'collective identity' for every argument so far. Those arguments related to meaning, knowledge, habitus, etc. – the fluid, interpretative, contextualized and changing facets of culture – might still hold true. However, arguments related to social structure, laws and regulations might not. At the end of the day, the world *is* clustered into nation states which are intertwined with supra-national institutions and spheres of regional and global economic integration, and it is these units that provide the frameworks for today's socio-economic, judicial and political structures (Cairns and Śliwa, 2008). For instance, national legal systems are only seldom subject to negotiation, and it therefore seems appropriate to investigate their cultural roots with macro-level tools, such as cultural dimensions or Kulturstandards (culture standards; see Chapter 2).

We could now say that collective identities cover subjective culture but do not cover every aspect of objective culture (see Chapter 3). This suggests that perceived sameness and differences across nations might have a structural (objective) and not an interpretative (subjective) root. Both should not be confused, as often happens. For example, many textbooks ascribe differences in work attitude, working hours, social cooperation to some permanent 'cultural attitude' or 'collective value', and not to the simple fact that there might be certain work regulations and laws encouraging a certain type of behaviour within a particular national environment (Tipton, 2008). Objective roots and national frameworks might also explain why some studies still identify distinct national cultural values (Minkov and Hofstede, 2012) or a shared political national culture (Chevrier, 2009) in multi-ethnic and multi-lingual nations.

To integrate multiple cultures and group-related identifications, CCM scholar Sonja Sackmann (1997) put forward the notion of 'cultural complexity'. This perspective acknowledges that individuals are part of many cultures, such as organizational, professional and team-based cultures, and that structural factors such as function, tenure and hierarchical position influence the configurations of culture (Sackmann, 1997: 3). The cultural complexity perspective also assumes that individuals might switch between multiple context-specific cultural identities.

Our sense of identity and how we recognize others also tend to be linked to mechanisms of power. For instance, social identity theory suggests that individuals tend to value their own group over others (Tajfel and Turner, 1986), a tendency which is called an 'in-group bias'. In the previous intercultural training example, HR managers truly believe that they are the only ones who know 'how to have a structured meeting', which makes them more socially competent than engineers. New HR managers learn these HR-identity requirements and how to express them, and are consecutively recognized as 'HR managers' by others. On the other hand, engineers have other identity requirements to consider, for example, 'being rational' based on the principles of mathematics and science, which lie at the core of 'global engineering identity' (Mahadevan, 2012a).

We can also assume that whereas collective identities are viewed as complementary, others are thought of as being mutually exclusive (Lawler, 2008), and both aspects might differ across how individuals view themselves and how others perceive them. Complementary collective identities are 'stacked upon each other'; they do not pose 'identity problems' in our own eyes or the eyes of others. For instance, if you are a male engineer *and* a long-distance runner, both identity facets might contribute to a required 'habitus of endurance' in engineering (see Chapter 1): they don't pose an identity problem, neither in your own eyes nor in the eyes of others, which means that your self-referencing and ascriptions by others overlap. However, if you are a *female* engineer and a long-distance runner, matters are more complicated, as you are now part of a gender minority in engineering. So maybe in your own eyes these three identity facets fit together, but clash in the eyes of some fellow (male) engineers or managers. Perhaps your competencies are undervalued when jobs are scarce: ascriptions by others create an identity problem where there is none for you.

Mutually exclusive identities are viewed as binary opposites, either by ourselves or by others, or by both parties. They lead to perceptions of irreconcilable difference (the *whole* identity is perceived as *completely* different). For instance, a female engineer might not 'feel at home' among fellow male engineers and may perceive her being female as opposite to her being an engineer. This constitutes an identity conflict on the level of self-referencing. Or fellow engineers might perceive a female engineer as a 'non-engineer' due to her gender. In this case, an identity conflict emerges from the ascriptions made by others. Last but not least, both mechanisms could come together.

Ascriptions by others are sometimes linked to their collective identity fears. Consecutively, the process of 'finding out what we have in common' (identity negotiation) might be obstructed, and 'identity wars' (fights over the 'better' or 'the only true' identity) could follow. For instance, if an engineer practises religion in the office, fellow engineers might perceive this as a threat to the identity requirement of a 'rational engineering'. As a result, they might react negatively and violently towards any religious expression at work, stop interacting with those practising religion and demand that religious beliefs be separated from engineering work (Mahadevan, 2012a).

Critical diversity and the mechanisms of difference

The previous considerations suggest that identity and recognition are more than just processes of self-referencing and ascriptions by others: they are a power mechanism, by which some differences are given more weight than others, and are used for defending or affirming people's own collective identity and status. To investigate these power effects, I suggest that CCM learn from critical diversity studies (P. Prasad, Pringle and Konrad, 2006). This might bring about a 'critical multiple cultures approach' to CCM. My argument departs from a simple inter-action, namely a handshake, from which we will deduce implications for diversity, identity and multiple cultures.

The handshake or when difference matters

This is a story of difference, as once experienced by me (in this case, a native German of mixed ethnicity with an Indian surname). It highlights how the meanings ascribed to a small difference create large and mutually-exclusive categories of difference. Difference then becomes reality; it *matters*. This is how the story goes.

Throughout my corporate life in Germany, I have worked in compa-nies or departments where 'shaking hands' was a formal ritual to be employed only during official customer visits or when meeting new people or corporate outsiders. All of these organizations were some-what 'young', cosmopolitan and sometimes highly technologized. What I had never encountered was entering the office in the mornings and doing a round of handshakes with everyone. This was something which I had only observed as an external consultant, mainly in small- and medium-sized German enterprises. To me, these companies seemed 'old', local and not high-tech, an etic perception which was obviously rooted in what seemed normal to me.

However, at a certain point in my life, I (again, a native German of mixed ethnicity with an Indian surname) became part of such a corporate culture myself and did not shake hands routinely in the mornings with everyone. Most of the time, I just forgot about this norm (which was not mine) and shouted an informal 'hi' or 'morning' to everyone present, as seemed appropriate to me. In retrospect, I reckon that it just did not occur to me to approach those working at their desks explicitly and individually, and – as it would seem to me – to 'force' them to stop what they were doing and shake hands. Even after I had become aware that this was the expected norm, it still felt like a strange, overly formal signal – it was just not 'me'.

You could now say that this is a simple thing: people have just learned slightly different ways of greeting each other at work, they will get over it, and that's that.

However, as it turned out, some of my colleagues began wondering about this new colleague of theirs (me). Questions circulated the office: 'maybe, it has something to do with her being an "Indian woman"?', some speculated. 'Maybe, it is a religious thing', others asked themselves. Around this time, I once entered the offices wearing an Indian-style embroidered shirt, and a few weeks thereafter, another colleague who hadn't been present that day told me that she had been told that 'Ms. so-and-so' (me again) 'is wearing a sari at work'. The sari is a female dress of South Asia consisting of a blouse and several yards of cloth draped around the body. My ethnic shirt was far from it, but also not too close to my mainly male co-workers' business-shirt-and-suit either.

After a few months, I had become a somewhat familiar face at the office. Still, one senior male colleague continued performing the follow-ing ritual on meeting me in bi-monthly formal project-team meetings. First, he would initiate a handshake, and then shy away in mock apology and say, 'oh, I am so sorry, I forgot that you don't shake hands'. After a few months of this play, I had become so annoyed by the whole thing that I made it a point *never* to shake hands with this colleague, and others would look on in wonder at our performance.

What might this example tell us about difference in CCM? First, it shows how processes of self-referencing and ascriptions made by others might diverge and create overwhelmingly different, mutually exclusive identities. The factual starting point is a small difference, namely slightly different interpretations of when and how to shake hands which originates from minor differences in regional, industrial, corporate, generational and potentially gender-related cultures within a single country: a difference that emerged from the normalities of social life. At this point, it could either have been unnoticed, or most likely, meaning would have been negotiated and somehow those involved would have become accustomed to each other. However, because this small phenomenon is exaggerated and ascribed to large markers of difference – societal culture, religion, etc. – it does not simply 'vanish' and instead becomes noteworthy. The handshake was *not* a big cultural rite at this company or an important symbol by which to express culture. It *became* big in the eyes of some and towards some, and those involved *made* it big.

After this process has started, other equally small cultural phenomena, such as a slightly ethnic choice of female dress, are interpreted as proof of this inflated, seemingly 'factual' difference. Over the course of time, strong feelings become attached to the symbol of the handshake. At a certain point and for some individuals, difference is not only a reality of life but becomes insurmountable and is made an object of a frontstage cultural 'play' (Goffman, 1959; see Chapter 1). This play involves performances of dominance (the male co-worker) and resistance (the new female employee); it reminds us that the relations of power, the meanings of difference and cultural contexts, are intertwined – a key point in the next chapter.

The handshake example suggests that specific contexts are shaped not only by perceptions of difference, but also by what perceptions of sameness and difference *mean* from the perspective of those involved, and which origins and categories perceived difference and sameness are ascribed to. This process emerges within specific boundary conditions and is at least partly open to negotiation. In the 'handshake example', I could either have been a young, cosmopolitan, female, German co-worker used to an informal corporate culture, or an 'Indian woman' who is somewhat 'religious'. The interpretative decision of others regarding this question will influence 'how I am perceived' in this context. This will influence my options of 'who I *can* be' and 'who I *want* to be'. Any negotiation of meaning will take place within these boundary conditions. It is at this point that difference starts to 'matter', and we can now say that what is perceived as a 'cross-cultural reality' is merely a by-product of it.

Ultimately, in uncertain interactions, we might simply have to 'risk' a positive and complementary interpretation of another person's identity – for we can never be sure whether our negative (etic) perceptions and the categories to which we ascribe difference are true or not. For instance, the new co-worker in the previous case (me), might either be a traditional 'foreigner' or an informal yuppie product of the internet revolution, and there can be no certainty of who this person *really* is, or if any of these labels are correct at all.

We can never know in advance the direction in which a context is going to develop: we will just have to leave the answer to this question open and continue investigating culture in context, based on the trust that all those involved will act with the best intentions.

The only way to make a context 'certain' is to project negative difference on the other person, and this might not be the most fruitful strategy. The negative labels chosen tend to be etic ones and might say more about those attaching them than about the person they are ascribed to. So, with regard to the 'handshake example', you might ask what motivates the established male colleague to invest time and effort in a regular front-stage play of difference, and why does the new co-worker react to this play?

Critical diversity and intercultural interactions

The previous examples suggest that there are two distinct conditions from which to approach collective identities in CCM, namely the perceived cultural middle (the majority perspective or cultural norm) and the cultural margins (the minority perspective or exception from the cultural norm). In the handshake example, it is the new co-worker who is not part of the cultural middle; in the global engineering example, it is female and/or offshore engineers.

When speaking of culture here, I understand it in the sense of 'what the relevant majority defines as collective identity in a specific context', not in the sense of 'what culture actually is'. For example, if maleness is the norm, then female constitutes the minority. If a certain religion is prevalent, then atheism or any other religion constitutes difference. As a result, certain minority members might be perceived as more alien than they actually are – they might be 'othered' (see Chapter 1). At the same time, members of the majority might cherish the feeling of being alike, and be 'saming' each other (just think of beliefs in a 'strong' and homogeneous national identity as opposed to presumably 'alien' immigrant communities). Both processes inform and legitimize each other, and in such a way, culturally relevant categories of sameness and difference are created and affirmed.

In the intercultural training example, engineers are *not* alike all over the globe, but might uphold this collective self-image to 'same' themselves against HR's exaggeration of national cultural differences. HR then becomes the respective 'other', and both interrelated perspectives and in-group biases are further affirmed (Mahadevan, 2011a). Likewise, the handshake is not a key symbol of organizational culture in the previous example, but triggered by the need to make sense of an unexpected minority practice, it *becomes* an important tool of identity-saming and of recognizing the 'majority identity' for some. Consecutively, some individuals – being perceived as a minority or different in the eyes of the majority – need to defend or prove their identities while others don't have to do so. This reminds us that the 'identity rules' required for recognition are not objective, and that only some set their terms.

Diversity literature often speaks of the 'Big 6' or 'Big 8' when considering relevant markers of difference. The Big 6 are gender, ethnicity (or race), age, ability, sexual orientation and religion (or worldview/ *Weltanschauung*); the Big 8 add other context-specific markers such as nationality or organizational role (see an overview in Plummer, 2003: 25; Bührmann, 2015: 23–42). Due to the fact that the Big 6 are part of many anti-discriminatory legal frameworks, e.g. in the European Union (Bendl, Eberherr and Mensi-Klarbach, 2012: 79), it seems sensible to concentrate on these when investigating critical diversity aspects of CCM. Studies suggest that companies and individuals at work have culturally learned to perceive these categories as dichotomist and to attach hierarchies to them, and that this might have critical implications (e.g. Tretheway, 2001; Ward and Winstanley, 2003; Zanoni et al., 2010; Acker, 2012; Levay, 2014; Mahadevan and Kilian-Yasin, 2016; Mik-Meyer, 2016).

For instance, it is generally assumed that individuals are born into the male and female 'sex', yet in biological reality combinations between the two do exist. Likewise, 'gender' describes the culturally-learned sense of behaviours and expectations which are mapped onto a specific 'sex' (Bührmann, 2015: 25). Please note again that culture has nothing to do with human biology. Still, an individual might be *perceived* as different in a negative way due to their ethnicity, race, gender, age, sexual orientation, and so on, and this makes critical diversity markers and their intersections culturally relevant. They therefore need to be considered for a critical CCM. For instance, if we find that female engineers are perceived as more incompetent than male engineers when jobs are scarce, we might need to question the dominant cultural meanings of 'competence' as related to dominant cultural meanings of 'female' and 'male'.

Likewise, it is often assumed that national belonging requires ethnic homogeneity, and this might disadvantage ethnic minority and migrant individuals at work (e.g. Van Laer and Janssens, 2011; Mahadevan and Kilian-Yasin, 2016). This also relates back to the 'Big 6' diversity dimensions themselves and how they are used. For instance, people tend to speak of 'race' in North American contexts, of 'ethnicity' in Western Europe, and of 'migration background' in countries such as Germany wherein the category 'race' is historically laden and national identification is rooted in presumed ethnic homogeneity (Mahadevan and Kilian-Yasin, 2016; Primecz, Mahadevan and Romani, 2016). This reminds us that the labels wherein we frame difference are linked to our own cultural glasses, even on scholarly level.

Still, not every perceived difference has power implications. For example, a friend of mine – an ethnic German, tall, blond, Nordic kind-of-guy – who lived and worked in the Silicon Valley and used to play badminton semi-professionally – was once the cause of the newspaper headline 'the first non-Asian guy to win the San Francisco Open'. Apparently, this was a relevant minority category when compared to the standard 'Asian-American badminton-playing type'. His partner in the men's doubles was also an internationally mobile highly-qualified corporate employee, a black Rastafarian from Jamaica. Both individuals were perceived as equally exotic on the badminton court; however, it was only the Rastafarian Jamaican who experienced being body-searched at airports when travelling internationally.

This suggests that the white, highly-educated German badminton player is merely excitingly different in a single context. For the Rastafarian Jamaican, the real-life consequences of being identified as a certain 'type' of individual by others weigh heavier and across more contexts. In international management, the implicit point of reference is the 'white, heterosexual, western, middle/upper class, able man' (Zanoni et al., 2010: 13), and the Rastafarian Jamaican, for example, cannot avoid being categorized in terms of race. Still, he is able to pursue an international career. This suggests that he, too, possesses sufficient symbolic and economic capital (see Chapter 1) which he can utilize to his advantage. He is also a majority member in terms of gender, and this might counterbalance other negative effects.

How to manage diversity is highly debated.[2] The business case for diversity proposes that the exclusion of parts of the workforce results in an inferior outcome. From this viewpoint, the Rastafarian Jamaican is not excluded. Another perspective assumes that advantaging some over others contradicts the assumption of merit-based organizations upon which, for instance, individual performance and employees' sense of fairness is based (*could* the Rastafarian Jamaican have achieved more?). Another argument originates from the simply human – or, as you might say, ethical – viewpoint that all human beings should have equal opportunities in the workplace and beyond. From this perspective, we might need to 'do something' about the international management environment experienced by the Rastafarian Jamaican or the female offshore engineers. (The internationally mobile German badminton-playing guy and the new female cosmopolitan co-worker seem safe.)

We also need to ask ourselves what it takes to overcome exclusion. Should we be colour-blind, that is treat everyone the same, or should we favour disadvantaged individuals over others (positive discrimination)? Critical diversity studies encourage the latter, based on the reasoning that exclusion is historical and systematic, that is long since rooted in the system, and that it takes a critical mass – a minimum number of minority individuals in certain positions – to overcome such effects (P. Prasad, Pringle and Konrad, 2006).

Some might now argue – for example, when finding arguments for who to body-search at airports – that 'statistics show' that 'this group' is 'more criminal' than another group, and countries might base the laws and regulations on this principle. Still, for a real person, this 'statistical approach' means; if you are unfortunate enough to be born 'black Jamaican', to express Rastafarian beliefs via your hairstyle, and to pursue an international career and travel a lot, then you might just have to live with being body-searched ('rules and regulations are nothing individual, after all ... '), and many might not question this principle. Ultimately, this 'statistical approach' would also lead to a 'well, if you are born female and choose to become an engineer, then you just have to live with a higher risk of being laid-off ... ', and at this point half of the world's population might disagree. This reminds us that, while we might have learned to view some marginalizations as more 'normal' than others, we *should* view all of them as what they are, namely unfair to the individuals whom they concern. Matters are complicated by the fact that some diversity makers are visible at first sight whereas others remain hidden or can be disclosed voluntarily (e.g. sexual orientation).

We should also bear in mind that most discrimination is implicit (and not explicit), which means that we cannot exactly pinpoint its origins and power effects, and that perspectives will diverge (what does the handshake example *mean* to whom?). For instance, a corporate ad might search for 'the best candidate' and not specify their ethnicity, but still, in the end, only candidates of the majority ethnicity might be selected. Whereas an ethnic minority member might view this as proof of discrimination, the ethnic majority might have the feeling that those selected are simply 'more competent' and not believe in ethnicity having any effect on their choices whatsoever (Holgersson et al., 2016). This presumed 'truth' might even prevail across national and organizational cultures (ibid.).

In some contexts, it might also be unclear what can be gained from higher diversity and how majority individuals might profit from it. It is often said that diverse teams are more innovative, yet they might also need to overcome higher initial obstacles to successful intra-team communication (finding a 'common way of doing and expressing things' is harder). Therefore, all team members must find the effort worthwhile, and again this tends to favour majority individuals over others. As conceptualizations of intercultural competence suggest (see Chapter 3), we need to be *motivated* to utilize the benefits of diversity, and this motivation needs to go deeper than purely economic arguments or individual interests. Otherwise, those who are not personally involved can afford to neglect matters of inclusion (because they themselves are included already) and might even sabotage efforts towards a more equal workplace (because competition, e.g. on the job market, might increase if previously disadvantaged groups are equally included).

These considerations enable us to see how intercultural interactions are not well balanced in the sense that two individuals meet on equal terms, and allow us to trace how one side might set the terms for the other. They also remind us that, if those who are advantaged (often the majority) think that you are different or don't belong, your ascribed difference and non-belonging might become a reality, regardless of how highly you score, for instance, on intercultural competence.

Approaching CCM via a critical diversity perspective highlights the need to look beyond an interaction itself in order to learn who is systemically, structurally and historically disadvantaged. It enables us to figure out which motivations and interests are attached to workplace diversity, and to include critical diversity markers such as race, gender, religion, ethnicity, sexual orientation, ableism, and so on in our cultural analyses. These are crucial contributions to a more 'equal' and 'fair' CCM practice, and we should not make do without them.

At the same time, we should also not become too sure of our 'critical' diversity categories. For instance, both white female candidates and non-white male candidates seem disadvantaged when it comes to top executive positions in Europe (Tienari et al., 2013; Holgersson et al., 2016). So whom to choose over the other? By making a choice, e.g. by supporting female minorities, corporate diversity policies might exclude ethnic male minority individuals (Tomlinson et al., 2013), and vice versa. In the end, a critical diversity practice, too, requires us to juggle and combine multiple viewpoints in order to make it more certain that our perspectives are fair and balanced, just like testing cultural dimensions in context (see Chapter 2) or negotiating meanings in intercultural interactions (see Chapter 3).

Identities beyond national culture

We can also approach critical diversity from another angle: most CCM theories and practices – this book included – implicitly assume that our lives evolve *within* national or societal identifications and that this is the starting point for how we experience culture. Still, we can observe that some individuals live and interact beyond national cultures. Biculturality is the most commonly used term for this phenomenon (Brannen and Thomas, 2010).

Individuals can be born into biculturality (e.g. children of a bicultural marriage) or become bicultural (e.g. via living abroad or being internationally mobile). Whereas some individuals might experience a high conflict between their different cultural identities, others might not, and both conditions can be favourable to bicultural competence. For instance, a perceived identity conflict, if dealt with, might result in higher reflexivity and cultural awareness (Brannen and Thomas, 2010). Bicultural and/or bilingual individuals are often able to access multiple interpretative frames and to 'span boundaries' across languages and cultures (Barner-Rasmussen, 2015). These bicultural competencies are assumed to be transferable across cultures in general (Brannen and Thomas, 2010).

Another phenomenon beyond national cultures is 'third culture kids', a term coined by John and Ruth Hill Useem (see Pollock and Van Reken, 1999). These are children of internationally mobile or migrant parents growing up in another cultural environment (Pollock and van Reken, 1999). It is assumed that 'third culture kids' retain influences from both the host and home country, but also develop something new and unique which emerges from the space between cultures.

Additionally, there are the 'global nomads' of today's business world, e.g. managers travelling a lot for work purposes, who experience a lot of cultures, yet might not do so in-depth. These are often viewed as high-performers to be considered for international top positions by corporate HR (e.g. Matthewman, 2011). Still, we might wonder whether these global nomads are truly beyond the dangers of a culturally unaware management? Maybe they just know the 'rules of global business' the best on an instrumental level.

Identities beyond national cultures are often described via hyphenate labels, such as 'Asian-Canadian', 'Japanese-Australian' or 'African-American'. This practice points to a 'halfie' identity (Abu-Lughod, 1991) and suggests that the majority of 'non-hyphenate' citizens (and maybe the 'halfies' themselves) cannot just 'let go' of categories of societal culture and national identity. Individuals with a 'halfie identity' tend to be perceived in terms of 'who they are not'. For instance, descendants of Turkish immigrants in Germany might be perceived as 'Turkish' in Germany and as 'German' in Turkey: each perspective, as shaped by the majority requirements for cultural belonging, perceives them as insufficient, while the whole of their identity, competencies, knowledge or skills remains unseen by most (Mahadevan, 2010).

Those living outside their country of origin, the so-called diaspora, tend to carry a version of their 'home-country culture' in their backpack that is different from the cultural developments there (S. Hall, 1990). Based on this understanding, Japanese immigrants and their descendants in Australia (a random example) do not live 'Japanese culture' as it is understood in Japan, but their own versions of it. They also live 'Australian culture', but combine multiple influences in new and creative ways.

At the same time, it could also happen that members of the diaspora live 'old' versions of the culture of their country of origin, particularly regarding highly symbolic rituals (see Chapter 3) such as marriage rites, family traditions or parent–child relations. These meanings and related behaviour of a certain era have been brought to the new environment and are now cut off from how those meanings changed in the country of origin. Because such meanings are highly symbolic and culturally relevant, members of the diaspora might be reluctant or unable to discard them; they pass on an 'older version' of culture which then changes into a new direction, based on the context-specific influences to which it is exposed. This means that any diaspora culture is a unique combination of 'new', 'old' and 'third' cultures, which informs and is informed by the cultures of the countries of origin and destination.

At work, the competencies of ethnic and migrant minorities tend to be undervalued (Syed, 2008; Syed and Özbilgin, 2009). For instance, Ingo Forstenlechner and Mohammed Al-Waqfi (2010) analysed discrimination as perceived by 40 first-generation Muslim ethnic minority employees and applicants in Germany and Austria. All interviewees perceived being discriminated against on the grounds of their 'being Muslim' and 'being ethnically different'. Interviewees also expressed the highest commitment at work when they did not feel discriminated against, although they had expected to be. This reminds us that discrimination is an emic reality in many individuals' lives, and that companies can profit from moving beyond it.

The very labels 'bicultural' or 'bilingual' affirm a dominant identity. Both terms, too, depart from the dominant assumption of a single cultural or linguistic identification and of a single national cultural belonging. Instead, 'halfie' might be the ironic self-description of those 'between cultures' when being faced with this perception, and I personally like this term the most.

Such a halfie identity might have its advantages, for it could well be that cultural awareness or intercultural competence are more easily possessed or achieved by those who experience episodes of 'otherness' or 'unfamiliarity' throughout their lives. To the halfies themselves, this might just be a seemingly 'normal' condition of their lives, but in anthropology, international business and management this is actually a highly-valued and sought-after competence. For instance, there are minority aspects in the lives of many prominent anthropologists, and this suggests that there is something to be learned from 'not fitting in' in the eyes of others and from being forced to 'deal with' questions of identity, recognition and belonging. Still, this, too, seems to require a conscious effort.

For example, a male German student of Turkish descent once told me that my class on diversity and identity was nothing new at all: 'But this is normal, my grandmother experiences this [being othered] every Ramadan in Germany!' This suggests that he was not aware that something very normal – namely, being perceived as a minority and having to juggle different requirements for belonging – was something that a person growing up in the 'cultural middle' might never have thought about or experienced themselves. This means that also a bicultural of 'halfie' life experience, if not reflected on, might be equally shaped by 'native categories' as any other social perspective. This suggests that individuals living in the cultural in-between are not 'automatically' interculturally or biculturally competent (Brannen and Thomas, 2010).

To develop a personal disposition into a conscious CCM tool, you (as a halfie) will need to become aware of what seems normal and make this explicit to others (not every migrant Turkish grandmother is a natural born cross-cultural manager). At the same time, a successful 'halfie manager' in a certain national or organizational culture might have climbed up the ladder not despite but *because* of their ability to adapt to the dominant identity requirements and hide their 'being halfie'. So maybe, at a certain point of a typical managerial career, there are not hidden 'bicultural' resources to tap into any more. This means that, whereas marginality, biculturality or partial otherness might be an advantage for a critical CCM and an ethnographic frame of mind, the same minority identity facets might be a disadvantage to purely national or inner-organizational management.

Globalization might not result in higher cultural homogeneity across the globe, as is often assumed, but instead an increasing variety of global and local ('glocal') combinations. Glocalization, a term made popular (but not invented) by Roland Robertson (e.g. Robertson, 1994), refers to the understanding that we can see the co-presence of universalizing and particularizing effects in today's (business) world. This is also called 'McDonaldization'. This fast-food chain exists in

many countries, it seems to offer a 'global' product and lifestyle, yet
that lifestyle is locally adapted (lamb-burgers in the Middle East, veg-
etable burgers and no beef in India, a blander taste in North America
and Western Europe). Therefore, glocalization is broadly the socio-
cultural equivalent to the business concepts of standardization versus
adaptation/localization. It suggests that individuals have more choices,
but that not everyone chooses the same. For example, in the 1980s
and 1990s you could not buy certain South-Indian spices in a city like
Munich, and acquaintances of South Indian descent would come back
from a trip to India loaded down with bags of spices. Nowadays you
can buy those spices in Munich, but it is unlikely that many would
wish to do so beyond the local South-Indian diasporic community.
Likewise, managerial styles across the globe might be characterized by
an increasingly individualized combination of more possibilities in
more contexts – yet management in general may not have become
more similar or 'global'.

In recent years, I have also experienced that local students in my
German CCM classes perceived themselves as inferior compared to
students who had spent a year abroad, who had travelled a lot in their
lives or who spoke excellent English. At the same time, nobody seemed
to admire students who spoke, let's say, Greek, Italian, Turkish or
Arabic with their parents at home. Also in management, it is more likely
that a white male candidate with a cosmopolitan life experience in the
English-speaking world is selected for a top executive position than an
ethnic non-white male migrant individual with roots outside the developed world (Holgersson et al., 2016).

This reminds us that not every international exposure is valued
equally, with cosmopolitanism perhaps being its most favourable version. Cosmopolitanism, that is 'identification' with the world in general,
has been suggested as an alternative to 'culture' in the sense of a single
territorial or national identification (Vertovec and Cohen, 2002).
Cosmopolitanism suggests that, at some point in the future, those of the
'cultural middle' and 'from one locality' are the ones who need to
defend themselves in the eyes of a rising cosmopolitan and 'beyond
national cultural' elite who will then be the ones dictating the terms of
culture. It remains to be seen whether this will be to the benefit of all
(Hannerz, 1990, 2004).

This insight introduces yet another perspective to the meanings of
difference. For example, the previous handshake example tells the
story of a bicultural and bilingual cosmopolitan female German (who
happens not to greet others as expected). One of her colleagues utilizes
this small difference in greeting habits for othering her. It might well
be that he does so out of his own fear of not meeting the requirements

of the shiningly new cosmopolitan 'managerial world' which this new co-worker represents. So, *could* it be that it is *he* who is the disadvantaged and undervalued individual in today's business?

Deconstruction and the need for more authentic acts of identification

In the end, we are all labelled by others and label others in return, and we cannot foresee the consequences of the identity labels involved. Although the specific mechanisms of exclusion might differ across contexts and individuals, diversity *always* seems to involve more favourable and less desired identities. This influences the differences we perceive, the meanings we give to difference and the categories to which we ascribe difference, and the ensuing implications for our identities and the identities of others.

For instance, throughout the previous chapters I have referred to scholars with the help of national and disciplinary 'identity labels', such as 'French sociologist Pierre Bourdieu'. Such a practice affirms single national identifications and cross-disciplinary difference and loses sight of alternative identity markers. Alternative labels would have been an option, for virtually all of these scholars have pursued an international career, lived in multiple countries and worked across disciplines. In some cases, I could not even come up with an appropriate disciplinary or national label, but once stuck with the principle I could not change the whole system. This reminds us that not only large discourses but also even the small and everyday labels we chose might become dominant and prescriptive (Näslund and Perner, 2011), and that we choose new labels within the frameworks of the choices we have already made and the labels which already exist. From now on, I am therefore going to refrain from scholarly labels in this book.

Still, non-labelling is also an implicit act of labelling, and all our choices of (non-) labelling have power implications. For instance, if I speak about 'manager xyz' and 'female manager abc', we can deduce that the male manager is the norm (for here, the identity tag 'male' is not added, it is the dominant category). If someone is explicitly labelled as the 'first African-American president', then we can infer that a 'white' 'US-American president' is considered the normality (if we assume that 'white' and 'black' are opposing racial social constructions), and we can deduce the power implications from there. At the same time, because we have not added the identity tag 'female', we should also assume that this individual is implicitly male.

'Reading between the lines' in such a manner is referred to as 'deconstruction' (based on Derrida, 1978; see also Critchley, 1992; Fougère and Moulettes, 2011).[3] Deconstruction is based on the assumption that we can deduce power implications and hierarchies from the choices of what is (not) said or done. It involves holding opposites in mind (e.g. ascribed categories of race), not only to understand how they differ but also to highlight how they are related (all our skins are coloured in an infinite number of shades): it is an act of interplay.

Via deconstructing established practice, we might question whether 'normal' labels and identity tags are actually representative of the person whom they concern (all labels are a somewhat arbitrary choice). So why is it that the label 'African-American president' was chosen over all other options, even though it might not be an accurate representation of the individual to whom it is attached? Bi-racial or multi-racial individuals are often categorically labelled 'non-white', despite their partly 'white' ancestry, and we can deduce hierarchies of 'whiteness' and 'non-whiteness' from this practice. We are therefore required to challenge the label 'black' and to question the power mechanisms by which it is attached.

Deconstruction also questions presumably power-free perspectives, such as 'emic' and 'etic' (see Chapter 3). In a multinational corporation or any competitive and profit-oriented environment where individuals need to succeed, identity and difference serve a *purpose*. The basic idea of CCM and intercultural competence is to increase the advantage of some over others, and the critical intersections in the intercultural training triangle point to these divergent motivations and interests on multiple levels. Who will triumph in the end is also a question of power, and of the ability to control and resist. This makes it seem even more relevant that we pay attention to the power-related *purposes* of CCM and intercultural interactions (control versus resistance) rather than solely differentiating between emic and etic (T. Jackson, 2013, 2014; based on L.T. Smith, 1999).

At this point, I would like to encourage you to research the life history of the 'first African-American president of the United States' and perform your own empirical act of 'imagining otherwise'. You could also try to deconstruct identity labels in your real-life interactions, or re-examine the previous handshake example. Such deconstructive acts might contribute to more authentic acts of identification. They could enable us to view others as 'who they are' – in their own terms – as far as possible and to see how they are not only different but also related. This allows us to become aware of the power implications of our patterns of identification and recognition, and to relate our managerial practice towards wider social requirements, such as fairness and equal opportunities. The following chapter builds on this thought.

Notes

1   There are other methods than intercultural training, for instance, intercultural coaching (an intercultural coach works together with a coachee in a long-term supportive process to develop individual capabilities), or intercultural team development (e.g. team members of a global team coming together in a joint activity). Still, preparatory intercultural training remains the standard tool in my experience, presumably due to cost-related reasons and the need to standardize training content in order to evaluate its return-on-investment.

2   The underlying sources to my discussion are *The Sage Handbook of Workplace Diversity* (edited by Alison M. Konrad, Pushkala Prasad and Judith K. Pringle, 2006); the *International Handbook on Diversity Management at Work* (edited by Alain Klarsfeld, 2010); and the *Routledge International Handbook of Diversity Studies* (edited by Steven Vertovec, 2015). This is also the reading I would recommend.

3   Deconstruction is linked to the postmodern paradigm (Alvesson and Deetz, 2000; Romani, Primecz and Bell, 2014). In contrast to positivism and interpretivism, postmodernism weighs the multiplicity, fluidity and heterogeneity of individual perspectives over the assumption of a shared and fairly homogeneous culture. Postmodernism presupposes multiple meanings, based on how individuals position themselves in relation to each other. These relations are understood as power relations, and this links postmodernism to the power-sensitive perspective on CCM (see Chapter 5).

5

Power and CCM

Building on the three sides of the CCM triangle, the previous chapter has investigated multiple cultures and collective identities within and beyond societal cultures. In particular, it highlighted the interlinkages between critical diversity categories, the dominance of single national cultural identifications, and intercultural interactions. It also proposed deconstructing these categories, for instance from the perspective of bi-cultural and halfie individuals. This chapter takes a wider lens and examines frameworks of power, and their origins and consequences for CCM; it is informed by critical and postcolonial thought (Jack and Westwood, 2009; Primecz, Mahadevan and Romani, 2016). It suggests that power is a part of potentially *all* CCM contexts, and that power is rooted in history and informs our knowledge. A discussion of the multiple facets of power therefore enables us to investigate CCM from a power-sensitive perspective.

Frameworks of power

Power is a paradox which is linked to the paradox of culture. On the one hand, power is permanent, fixed and exists 'somewhere'. We can identify laws, rules and regulations, and there are certain individuals or institutions, such as 'the police', who are entitled to enforce 'the law'. This suggests that there is something like 'objective' power, which involves a source and someone or something towards whom or which power is directed.

On the other hand, power is also fuzzy and subject to negotiation; we cannot really grasp it, it emerges somehow, and it might not be clear from where and towards whom power manifests itself. For example, if a group of people starts cooperating, certain conventions of who does what, who speaks when and so on, emerge. But where do they emerge *from*? Sometimes, roles, routines and regulations pre-structure the interaction, but more often, group processes just 'happen'. They involve the dominance of some over others, acceptance of or resistance towards being dominated, and the general possibility to change these interactions. When we interact this way, we relate back to what is known, what has been experienced before, what seems to make sense, and so on, and when 'enacting power', we are influenced by practices and interpretations which already exist. So, are we free to act, or do pre-existing ideas of 'how things work' or 'what power looks like' pre-determine our choices? To answer these questions, we will need to juggle different concepts of power, particularly the interrelated elements of discourse, structure, practice and agency.

Structure, practice and agency as circuits of power

Structure, practice and agency are related and intertwined angles from which to investigate culture and power. In *Frameworks of Power*, Stuart Clegg (1989) suggests that we can understand these three aspects as 'flows of power' (which means that power is not fixed and stable but is a socio-cultural process) that are interconnected as 'circuits of power' (they can be switched on and off). The 'switches' for these circuits of power are the so-called 'obligatory passage points'. You can think of them as the central train station through which all suburban trains, regardless of their direction, speed, number of passengers etc., need to pass on their way in and out, stopping briefly or for a more extended period on the way.

A structural perspective on power assumes that it is institutionalized in social structures, norms and regulations, and that we cannot or can only partly escape these power effects in our practice: a formalized train schedule determining individual travel.

Agency can be understood as our individual ability to overcome, change, subvert or otherwise influence systems of power (Foucault and Gordon, 1980): it is about our individual ability to resist dominance (Clegg, 1989). We do so by positioning ourselves towards others and when interacting with them. So, individuals can use other means of transport than the suburban trains, if the timetable does not fit their interests. They might even rally and interest others in, for instance, forming carpools, and by enlarging the group of those resisting the system they might render the suburban train lines passengerless, which puts pressure on the schedule to change.

Rules of practice link structure and agency. They fixate social meaning and membership, that is they determine what things mean and who belongs to a certain group, and this is their power (Clegg, 1989). For example, each company has structural regulations regarding working hours (full flexibility is a regulation as well). Still, in every company there are 'loopholes' to escape regulations: individuals have agency. They might even bring about a new practice or new structural regulations. Structure and agency meet in rules of practice. For instance, are individuals laid off when opposing working-hours regulations or is this a common practice ignored by those in charge?

CCM contexts as nodes of power

How and when is each circuit of power – structure, practice or agency – switched on or off (to speak in engineering terms)? This is decided via obligatory passage points (Clegg, 1989) which we can understand as 'nodes of power' that all flows of power need to pass through (based on Callon, 1986; Clegg, 1989). For a power-sensitive CCM, you can best understand a 'node of power' as any social interaction, situation, phenomenon or experience from which we can unravel power effects. If we suspect that a certain individual is marginalized in CCM, we cannot argue with power discrepancies *in general*, but only as emerging from a *particular* context which concerns specific individuals in specific situations informed by specific frameworks of power.

For example, in Chapter 4 we briefly encountered a black Rastafarian Jamaican working in Silicon Valley (actually, as the CEO of a technology-intensive company) who travelled internationally and was body-searched on no *particular* grounds whatsoever. We can now investigate this experience in terms of structure (e.g. airport regulations and passport requirements), practice (e.g. what officers actually do and how often the CEO travels) and agency (e.g. customs officers' ability to restrict the CEO's travels versus the CEO's ability to resist), the key question being whether individual agency is restricted by dominant structures and practices. On the other hand, we should also acknowledge that agency manifests itself in multiple ways. The Rastafarian Jamaican CEO, for instance, took pictures of those airport hubs where he was body-searched or even detained, and exhibited (and partly sold) these photographs successfully. By doing so, he might have changed perceptions, which might change practice, and maybe even structures.

This suggests that no power relations are absolute: they leave room for interpretation and individual choice, and individuals might have agency to change, resist and subvert the system and to introduce new meaning. On the other hand, power discrepancies *do* limit individual choice, and individuals might be subjected to imbalances of power. Providing the link between structure and agency, rules of practice might help us identify who belongs and who does not, who is recognized as part of the 'we' and who is labelled as 'different'.

In the end, any interaction might be a 'node of power', and this means that we cannot assume it is solely the participants' intercultural competence which determines the outcome of the interaction (see Chapter 3). We can now begin to categorize intercultural interactions in terms of structure, practice and agency, and try to infer categories and patterns from this context.

This adds to our understanding of how to investigate CCM contexts. Previously, we have encountered the requirements to test hypotheses in context and from an ethnographic frame of mind (Chapter 2), to pay attention to how meaning is negotiated in intercultural interactions (Chapter 3), or to move back and forth between multiple perspectives on diversity and identity (Chapter 4). If doing so from a power-sensitive perspective, we might see whether, in which context and to what extent structure dominates, or whether, in which context or to what extent individuals successfully resist, change and subvert the system via agency. Most likely, reality will not be a clear-cut 'either–or' but a complex interplay between structure and agency through practice.

The power of discourse

All three circuits of power are intertwined with discourse. Discourses are 'ideas about reality' which also *are* a reality. Discourses exist 'somewhere', yet we can never pinpoint their exact source. For instance, where does the presumed 'logic' to body-search a black Rastafarian Jamaican CEO as opposed to a white US-American CEO originate from?

Discourses also require certain 'practices of their production, dissemination, and reception' (cf. Phillips and Hardy, 2002: 3; based on Parker, 1992), and this way they 'bring an object into being'. For example, the Rastafarian Jamaican is more often body-searched than a representative of another 'type' of frequent traveller. This practice makes the 'picture' become a fact which further informs how the world is perceived – other travellers will observe the Rastafarian Jamaican being led away to be body-searched. This way, discourse categorizes our interpretations; it 'hovers' above our life experiences and sometimes touches upon them.

'Normal' discourses, like culture, are at least partially open to interpretation; they have multiple meanings and can change over time. We therefore need to assume that not *everyone* promotes the same perceptions or attaches the same meanings to a concept. For example, although most people have heard of the terms 'ethics' or 'human rights', these terms might mean different things to different individuals, they will be put into practice differently in different organizational and societal contexts, and they are even institutionalized in different ways (is the death penalty ethical or not?). So, again, human beings are producers and products of discourse.

Still, some perceptions become dominant on the levels of structure and practice, and certain individuals seem to have more room for agency than others. Or, as you might say, some discourses are linked to 'particular power techniques' (Alvesson and Deetz, 2006: 266), for instance, the practice only to body-search a certain *type* of individual.

Dominant discourses marginalize or even silence alternative interpretations and practices (Phillips and Hardy, 2002). For example, in the 1950s and 1960s, women from many cultural contexts – for instance, the great film divas of the day – wore a headscarf. At that point in time, the headscarf carried multiple symbolic meanings, such as a practical piece of clothing, a glamorous accessory, a practice of modesty across religions, and so on. This points to an open, potentially changing and multifaceted 'normal' discourse.

Nowadays, the female headscarf is almost exclusively interpreted as a religious symbol (veil) which signals Muslim and 'non-Western' identity (Primecz, Mahadevan and Romani, 2016). Predominantly negative meanings are attached to it, such as exaggerated religiousness, traditional backwardness and female oppression (Golnaraghi and Dye, 2016), and those wearing it in 'Western' managerial contexts risk suspicion and marginalization (Essers and Benschop, 2009; Golnaraghi and Dye, 2016). Pushkala Prasad (2012: 69, cf. Golnaraghi and Mills, 2017) writes about how the discourse of the veil has immediate effects on Muslim women at work: 'Most strikingly, it [the discourse of the veil] mediates a range of personnel practices from hiring criteria to organizational dress codes that exclude and marginalise Muslim immigrants and their descendants'. This suggests that wearing the veil might make a difference to a Muslim woman's opportunities at work.

We can therefore say that dominant discourse transformed a piece of cloth into what Erving Goffman (1963) has called a 'stigma symbol'. Stigma symbols are different from 'normal' symbols as they can hardly be negotiated or re-interpreted anymore. 'Normal' symbols *ask* you to give your own meanings to them, and their interpretation is heterogeneous. Stigma symbols are prescriptive and fix singular meanings. They *tell* you what you *should* think and feel about them, and this mechanism overshadows the unbiased negotiation of meaning and changes practice (women might think twice before wearing a headscarf to protect themselves from the rain, for example). So can a CCM interaction involving a veiled woman *really* be independent of dominant discourse?

To establish a non-discriminatory and non-stereotyping CCM practice we need power-sensitive tools – for instance, the ability to look back onto dominant discourses. In the previous example, dominant discourse is rooted in the implicit assumption that the 'Western' woman is more liberated than the 'Muslim' woman (A. Prasad, 2006). If we look at this belief from an alternative angle, we need to consider that one of the arguments in favour of wearing the Muslim veil or body veil is that, by being hidden, the female body is actually *less* discriminated against. From a critical viewpoint, male perspectives on women, for instance, regarding the female body, are mechanisms by which women are disciplined. In contexts wherein men are dominant, e.g. management, women are therefore required to present a female body which meets the expectations of the male majority in order to be perceived as competent (Tretheway, 1999). If viewed from this perspective, a *veiled* body, which hides the female body from the eyes of men, might actually be a vehicle for escaping male dominance (Primecz, Mahadevan and Romani, 2016). By at least considering this alternative viewpoint, 'Western' cross-cultural managers might learn about their blind spots.

Dominant discourses and counter-discourses are often linked to perceived mutually exclusive identities. For instance, if you ask the imagined 'Western European (wo)man on the street': 'can one be a European Union (EU) citizen and Buddhist?', you might get answers such as: 'How should I know? Never thought about it; don't know any Buddhists'. However, if you ask the same imagined 'Western European (wo)man on the street' 'can one be a EU citizen and Muslim?', you might get 'Yes' and 'No' answers and heated debates. Obviously, these statements of mine are not based on rigorously collected data, they just originate from discussions I had and observations I made. So maybe my perception is wrong, but it seems that there is a dominant discourse in the shape of a question, namely 'does Islam belong to Western Europe?', and if this is the case, then people will have opinions on the matter. Simply speaking, if we believe that 'this is what things mean', and if we act accordingly, then 'this is what things *will* mean'. Whenever you stumble on a heated 'Yes'-and-'No' debate, or the perception of 'them' versus 'us', you have most likely hit upon such dominant discourse, which tends to be linked to the identity fears of one or either party.

Power and knowledge: imagined geographies in CCM

Discourses inform us that power and knowledge are interlinked. This implies that no knowledge is 'objective' or 'power-free'.[1] For example, people often speak of 'the West' and seem to know what 'the West' is (you could therefore call 'the West' a 'discourse'). But why is it that a country such as Egypt is considered 'the non-West', whereas a country such as Australia is considered 'the West'? Egypt lies in close proximity to what is labelled 'Western Europe', on a Western meridian, whereas Australia is located in the Southern Hemisphere, on an Eastern meridian, and at roughly the same degree of longitude as, for instance, Japan, which is perceived as a part of 'the Far East'. And what is the standpoint from which to locate two-dimensional directions such as 'East' and 'West' on a three-dimensional sphere? The only factual geographical 'rule' for locating 'East' and 'West' is the Greenwich zero meridian, but why should an English suburban town be the perspective from which to view the world?

The answers to these questions are unsatisfying on a factual level, and this suggests that 'West' and 'non-West' are not objective and 'true' geographical units but, in the words of Edward Said (1979: 357), the product of 'imagined' or 'imaginative geography': we have *learned* to view the globe this way, and this view has created certain realities.

Depending on the perspective taken, 'the non-West' in CCM either means 'the Asian East' or 'the Orient'. 'The Asian East' is the presumably 'ancient' cultures of India and Greater China.[2] In intercultural training practice and corporate human resource development strategy, these countries are often portrayed as 'traditional' and 'exotic' (that is, limited by culture) and judged against an apparently more enlightened, rational and non-traditional management style practised in 'the West', which is thought of as culture-free or culturally-superior (Mahadevan, Müller and Pauer, 2012).

Alternatively, 'the non-West' in CCM might signify 'the Orient', which is subjected to a discourse called Orientalism (Said, 1979). Orientalist discourse portrays 'the Arab world' and Islam not as they are but as what 'the West' is not. For example, whereas 'the West' is perceived as rational, enlightened, modern and secular, 'the Orient' is viewed as emotional, unenlightened, traditional and religious. Whereas 'the West' is ethical and lawful, 'the Orient' is portrayed as sinful and despotic. 'The Orient' serves merely to define 'the West' – it is only via imaginations of what is 'Oriental' that we can understand what it means to be 'Western'. Naturally, within Orientalist discourse, 'the West' possesses superior qualities. You can think of this mechanism as the intercultural trainers' need to 'prove' cross-cultural difference in order to affirm themselves as the superior experts in overcoming it (see Chapter 4).

The categories 'Global North' and 'Global South' (Wallerstein, 1974) are slightly different yet related concepts from which to investigate power in context. On a factual level, they describe the observation that if we classify the world into categories such as 'developed' and 'developing nations', a larger number of developed nations can be found in the Northern Hemisphere. Obviously, you could question the categorization of developed versus developing nations as ethnocentrist, as it measures what 'the West' excels at, and you could ask yourself where the resources for Western development actually came from (for example, from colonial exploitation of 'the non-West'; see Cairns and Śliwa, 2008, in this series). However, even if we accept this categorization of the world, then 'Global North and South' are more than geographical facts but imagined categories. For instance, Australia and New Zealand are part of the Global North despite their location on the Southern Hemisphere. On the other hand, a country such as Japan is still part of 'the non-West', even though it is 'developed'.

We should therefore keep in mind that the categories of 'the non-West' and 'Global South' only emerge when the world is perceived through the eyes of 'the West', understood as 'the developed world'. This viewpoint constructs 'the non-West'/'Global South' as inferior and in terms of how they are 'not yet Western' or 'developed'. For example, it is often assumed that 'modern' managerial theories and methods originate from 'the West' and need to be introduced to 'the non-West' (Cooke, 2004). Whereas 'Western' theories and methods are imagined as being 'modern' and having global implications, so-called 'indigenous' theories and methods are considered to be 'traditional' and helpful only for the local context from which they emerge (T. Jackson, 2013, 2014). The failure to implement Western strategy at non-Western sites is often explained with the traditionalist local culture (Cooke, 2004).

Attached to this differentiation is an implicit discourse of 'help' or 'developmental aid' which presupposes that the 'non-Western' countries of the 'Global South' are in need of Western help and education (overview in Ziai, 2016). The whole developmental aid business could be questioned from this perspective. It tends to create passive recipients of Western altruism which actually might just be another form of cultural imperialism or dominance. This dichotomy also presupposes that it is only 'the non-West' or 'Global South' that can learn from 'the developed West', and it remains unthinkable that 'the non-Western Global South' might contribute or possess knowledge and know-how in its own right. You can think of this mechanism as a HR manager's implicit assumption that engineers for whom HR has scheduled an intercultural training *must* be culturally unaware if they reject this training on the grounds that they don't experience cross-cultural differences in engineering (see Chapter 4). By categorizing engineers in terms which support HR claims to power and knowledge, HR managers construct engineers not only as different within an HR worldview but also as *inferior*. The same kind of thinking tends to be applied by 'Western' managers to individuals from 'the non-Western Global South'.

We can identify multiple shortcomings of imaginative geographical categories, for instance ethnocentrism, stereotyping, othering, marginalization, neglect of cultural heterogeneity and change, naïve realism and native categories (see Chapter 1). Nonetheless, the categories of 'West' and 'non-West', as well as 'Global North and South', seem to be omnipresent, as is the labelling of individuals in these terms. This practice is problematic, for it creates mutually exclusive identities (see Chapter 4), obstructs commonalities and constructs individuals as fundamentally different from 'the West' and 'the developed world'.

CCM operates within and contributes to these discursive categories. For example, it is routinely assumed that it is the Western, white and often male manager who needs to manage non-Western, non-white subordinates abroad (Primecz, Mahadevan and Romani, 2016). Training material, textbooks, case-study examples, critical incidents, role plays and textbooks implicitly place this archetype centre stage, and you might well examine your own study material in this light. These implicit hierarchies in international management might contribute to the social stratification of the expatriate class. For example, Françoise Goxe and Marjolaine Paris (2016) examine the phenomenon that the top executives of a European company in Nigeria are from Europe, whereas lower positions are occupied by managers from non-first-world countries. They show that the various forms of capital (social, cultural, economic and symbolic) influencing the career mobility and the organizational status available to these expatriates are rooted in how 'desirable' their country of origin is from the dominant perspective. This way, imaginative geographical hierarchies shape and constrain individual careers.

So is 'the modern West' merely a construction, or is there more to it? At this point, history becomes relevant to CCM practice. For instance, for a certain period, the British Empire covered more than one third of the globe, and this explains why English has emerged as the global *lingua franca* of international business and management. Likewise, the Greenwich zero meridian is a product of previous English naval and territorial dominance. This suggests that certain business 'normalities' and our presumed 'knowledge of the world' tend to be rooted in actual historical developments such as colonialism and imperialism. To become aware of the categories and structures wherein we think, feel and act, we therefore need to examine history as related to all circuits of power (including discourse) and as informing our 'knowledge' of the world.

▰▰▰▰ Colonialism and imperialism: the historic roots of power/knowledge

Colonialism was a period lasting from the 15th century to the mid-20th century, during which European powers established colonies in other parts of the world (Cairns and Śliwa, 2008). Economic interests, for instance access to raw materials and goods, or strengthening home economics via the policy of mercantilism, were often the first step towards territorial expansion (Osterhammel, 2005).

It is often suggested that the political acquisition of colonies was simply a by-product of the need to secure trade (Osterhammel, 2005), and indeed the first organizations acting globally were trading companies such as the British East India Company or the Dutch *Vereenigde Oostindische Compagnie* (VOC) intending to secure the trading of spices, pepper, and other goods with what are today India and Indonesia (Cairns and Śliwa, 2008). Sometimes these organizations were welcomed by local and often rival rulers, who tried to exploit the supreme military power of these companies in their own interests. Ultimately, trading companies became political bodies and the territories governed by them fell under crown control. Ensuing British rule in India or Dutch rule in what is today Indonesia never covered the whole of these territories, but was mainly meant to secure trade and economic interests and exercise political and administrative control (Majumdar, Raychaudhuri and Datta, 1978: 623–822; D.G.E. Hall, 1981).

Imperialism literally refers to the goal and practice of creating an empire (from the Latin, *imperium*), and therefore to any historical development of such a kind, be it the Inca, the Mali or the Roman Empire. However, in its current usage 'imperialism' has mainly come to refer to conditions in 19th- and 20th-century Europe (including Britain), and their consequences for the relations between Europe and other continents. Additionally, the term might also refer to Japanese and US-American expansionist policy, mainly lasting from the late 19th to the mid-20th century.

Imperialism involves a sense of the superiority of the 'white race' (Hobson, 1902), as, for example, Rudyard Kipling's famous (1899) poem 'Take Up the White Man's Burden' suggests, by which he meant to encourage the US to follow the European imperialist tradition and take up the 'burden of empire' (mainly concerning the Philippines). In order to trace the legacies of imperialism, we might best consider it in a wider sense, that is, on the level of informal flows of trade, migration or capital, rather than narrowing it down to formal empires (e.g. Said, 1993). For example, as John Gallagher and Ronald Robinson

(1953) have suggested, the principle of free trade is an imperialist practice: it enabled industrialized nations to secure their historical advantage in world business (Cairns and Śliwa, 2008).

Colonialism and imperialism are overlapping concepts (Gilmartin, 2009), albeit with slightly different focus points (e.g. Hobsbawm, 1989; Howe, 2002). Imperialism has a more political connotation and can be defined as 'a system of power, political economic ascendancy and cultural subordination, envisioned from the centre of expanding nation-states and differentially operationalized in colonized spaces throughout the world' (Morrissey, 2014: 17–18). Colonialism, as the more business-related concept, involves (1) relations between a minority of foreign invaders and a local majority, (2) decisions which are made by the minority in the interest of their home country but affect the majority, and (3) a sense of mission and supremacy on the colonizers' side (Osterhammel, 2005: 16).

In the terminology of this book, these definitions of colonialism/ imperialism involve the interrelated levels of discourse (how we refer to something, and how this in return structures the way in which the world is perceived), structure (the frameworks, institutions, economic policies, laws, etc. which are created in order to implement this world-view), and practice (how individuals act within these structures and relate to these concepts). We also need to assume that such power effects can never be absolute, because there is scope for agency (the individual power to resist and change a system).

Colonialism and imperialism, and their power implications, are relevant to CCM today because we might identify contemporary contexts, discourses and frameworks which are characterized by similar power-discrepancies. These are called neo-colonial ('newly colonial') or neo-imperialist (Banerjee and A. Prasad, 2008; Boussebaa and Morgan, 2014), and the discourse on the Muslim veil (see above) provides an example. In Canada, for instance, the media promote a strong opinion against the veil, especially the full-body and full-face veil (*niqab*). Golnaz Golnaraghi and Kelly Dye (2016) identify this opinion as rooted in the neo-colonial discourse that veiled women – as viewed through the eyes of 'the West' – are overly religious and traditional, oppressed by (Muslim) men and in need of being saved (by the West). The prescribed means for doing so are 'Western' democracy and liberality, and of course choosing not to wear the veil. This is a neo-imperialist worldview that values the 'Western' way of life over other orientations. As Henriett Primecz, Jasmin Mahadevan and Laurence Romani (2016) conclude, 'In consequence, in cross-cultural management contexts involving a veiled woman, others are likely to project this (neo-) colonial view on her'. At the same time, the presumed 'homogeneous way of

Western life' within this discourse is a mere collective imagination and construction as well. It serves to differentiate 'the West' from 'the Orient' and defines the 'Western' superior purpose – namely to free, develop and modernize 'the Orient'.

Colonial legacies go beyond the actual context of colonization (de l'Estoile, 2008: 268), and they also involve countries and regions without an actual colonial past (Canada had no overseas colonies). For example, colonialism and imperialism introduced a specific direction for the flow of managerial and organizational knowledge, namely from the centre to the periphery (Wallerstein, 1974; Frenkel and Shenhav, 2006),[3] with the Global North/West broadly representing the 'centre' and the Global South/non-West occupying the periphery.

For instance, Germany is a country without an actual colonial past (or only a 'short' or 'failed' colonial past). Still, a German high-tech company offshoring and outsourcing standardized work packages to India might be considered neo-colonial and neo-imperialist (Mahadevan, 2011a, 2015a), as control from the centre is exercised over the periphery. Resources at the periphery (Indian engineers) are not the ones setting the terms of this relationship: they are not the ones to define corporate strategy or develop technical innovations and are reduced to implementing headquarter designs and specifications. As there is also a German self-image of being a country of 'good engineering', dominant discourse is in line with dominant structure (headquarters–subsidiary relations): German engineers might truly believe that they are better engineers than their Indian counterparts, and might also feel the need to educate them without feeling the need to change themselves or reflect upon their own viewpoints. They might even think that it is their responsibility to supervise the Indian engineers as they are less developed and qualified compared to the perceived 'German engineering expert' (German engineers 'take up the White man's burden').

Other historical developments which might create neo-colonial/ neo-imperial contexts and frameworks are, for instance, the legacies of the Cold War (international business is 'capitalist') or the hegemonic geo-politics after World War II (Szkudlarek, 2009; T. Jackson, 2011). For example, scholars have pointed out that US-American dominance in international management and business has also been brought forward by the country's 'commercial-military-political complex' (Westwood and Jack, 2008). Consequently, textbooks tend to take a dominant image of US-American culture as the implicit point of reference, and assume that every society and economic system will either modernize in this direction or stagnate as 'failed Americans' (Tipton, 2008).

In such neo-colonial or neo-imperialist CCM contexts, critical diversity implications are to be expected (see Chapter 4), and it becomes unlikely that those in intercultural interactions will meet on equal terms (see Chapter 3). To overcome these biases, we therefore need to treat historic developments such as colonialism and imperialism not as finite historical events but as a present and future source of knowledge/power that informs our CCM practice and shapes the structures wherein our intercultural interactions take place.

What does history *mean* for CCM? An interplay

Power is a paradox, which means that the power of history to determine our actions cannot be absolute. So what does history *mean* for CCM today? Has it created dominant hierarchies (rooted in discourse, structure and practice) which cannot be overcome, or do individuals have the agency to resist and subvert an unequal system? How *exactly* do discourse, structure, practice and agency come together in a potentially neo-colonial and neo-imperialist managerial world?

Neo-colonial discourses, structures and practice remain dominant

On the one hand, we could say that imperialism and colonialism transmitted discourses, structures and practices which created power discrepancies in international business and management. Imagined geographical categories such as 'West' and 'non-West' are one example of how dominant discourses manifest in dominant structures and practices.

We might even say that these mechanisms are so fundamental that we cannot escape them. For example, the concept of the nation state, with its implicit assumptions of ethnic homogeneity and a single national language, is an 'invention' of 19th-century Europe. Prior to it, many individuals throughout Europe were bi- or multi-lingual. Those at the borders of today's nation states might not even have spoken the 'high' language of the nations of which they are part today but rather may have shared the same dialect (e.g. Frisian or Alemannic). Colonialism and imperialism made the nation state a globally dominant discourse, structure and practice which do not fit the whole of the world, and that is a structural and dominant imbalance of power. For example, if you consult a map, you will see surprisingly straight national demarcation lines in some regions of the world, such as on the African continent. These were often drawn by colonial powers on the negotiation table in order to separate their respective colonial spheres of influence, or – based on the imperialist principle of *divide et impera* (Latin for divide and rule) – cut across indigenous territories to secure colonial dominance. From a structural perspective, we therefore *must* assume that these nations might be historically disadvantaged, and that this disadvantage is 'built into' the system of the world.

At the same time, we can also assume that, despite dominant structures and practices, the meanings of 'the nation state' might vary from context to context. Take Indonesia, for instance, with hundreds of indigenous languages and Malay as an 'imported' national language. There is also India, a whole subcontinent of different histories, with more than 1.2 billion inhabitants of various ethnicities and the English language as the shared economic *lingua franca*. Do nationality and national frameworks really *mean* the same from an Indonesian or Indian perspective?

We will also find room for agency. In some regions, nomadic ethnic groups, such as Bedouins of Northern Africa, resist artificial national borders and routinely travel across them.

Still, this does not make the Bedouin way of living equal, as it is to be assumed that someone living this alternative concept will not make her/his way up the managerial ladder in a Western multinational company. Also, the Indonesian or Indian (or Cameroonian, Nigerian, Guatemalan, and so on) life experiences of a multi-ethnic, multi-lingual, multicultural nation state have not found their way into CCM literature. Tools such as cultural dimensions which presume a certain – 'European' – type of nation state (ethnically and linguistically homogeneous) are still the dominant global tool for investigating national cultures. In this way, even alternative meanings and acts of resistance remain marginalized and affirm dominant structures, practices and discourses involuntarily.

Nonetheless, cultural flows are translated and appropriated

Still, we can also see that the relations between colonizers and colonized were not a one-way process, and this makes colonization also a story of agency. For example, the British in India trained Indians as administrative middlemen (with a flow of knowledge from the colonizers to those being colonized). Some Indians received crucial colonial knowledge and gained access to higher English language education, which was essential to the colonial apparatus. Indians trained as administrative middlemen were then 'exported' to other parts of the British Empire. In many colonies a racialized colonial society emerged, with Englishmen at the top, Indians in the middle, and – if outside India – the local population at the bottom (Furnivall, 1956). As a result, ethnic Indians today live in many parts of the world, for example in South Africa, the Caribbean, Southeast Asia[4] and former British colonies in Africa. The Indian independence movement leader M.K. Gandhi (mostly referred to as 'Mahatma', an honorific title meaning 'great soul') practised law in South Africa, having obtained his degree in England, prior to committing himself to the civil rights movement. Ultimately, India became independent as a nation after World War II, with English as a *lingua franca*, a political, administrative and educational system modelled after the British example, and an extensive railway infrastructure built by the British. This reminds us that colonialism and imperialism not only categorized and separated individuals in asymmetrical relations, but also resulted in *cultural flows* beyond and across these categories. In some countries, such as India, we cannot separate both.

We can also see that individuals seem to have the power to change and subvert a system. For example, cricket is *the* Indian national sport today, a remnant of English colonialism. Yet, what cricket 'means' in the Indian context is very much different from its former meaning as an upper-class leisure activity for English gentlemen. In India today, cricket is a national sport for amateurs and an event similar to soccer in Europe and the UK (Appadurai, 1995). This tells us that cultural flows are linked to cultural translation ('changing meaning') and appropriation ('making a system of thought and related practices your own'). In the process, new discursive meanings emerge.

To understand processes of appropriation, Homi K. Bhabha has coined the term 'mimicry' (1994). In biology, mimicry refers to a form of mirroring without understanding (as when apes mimic human behaviour). Reinterpreting this term for a critical analysis of colonial legacies, Bhabha suggests a two-fold process: a practice is first copied and then given new meaning.

We can even observe that cultural meanings might 'travel back' to their origins. For example, Bollywood movies in India have been influenced by pictures of 'the West' transported by Hollywood movies (the globally dominant movie source against which all other movie industries therefore measure themselves), and they transport these – translated and appropriated – meanings to a local Indian audience. However, watching Bollywood movies has also become popular in many Western countries. Now, these meanings travel back (to the dominant source) and are assumed to transport an image of 'what India is like' (which was not their purpose), and a process of 'counter-translation' begins. In such a manner, those colonized might 'speak back'.

Often, appropriation takes place in 'third spaces' (Bhabha, 1990: 38.) These are spaces wherein the translation and negotiation of cultural meanings take place, resulting in new cultural combinations. In the past, this might have been interactions in the colonial administration. Nowadays, a third space might be found among international managers in a multinational corporation (Frenkel, 2008). You could also say that an English language CCM class in an international study programme in a non-English-speaking environment is a 'third space'.

From an agency-oriented perspective, the outcome of cultural flows and processes of translation and appropriation cannot be prescribed. For example, corporate meaning travels across national cultures, and those receiving it recontextualize it in unforeseen ways, as the (near) failure of Disneyland in Paris and its success in Tokyo suggest (Brannen, 2004).

But still, some of us are historically and presently excluded

Nonetheless, we should not assume that everyone is equal just because we all (potentially) have the agency to re-contextualize, translate and appropriate cultural flows. For instance, does it *really* make no difference at all if a slim and fit, male, ethnic Caucasian, natural-born US-American and a slightly obese, female, non-white migrant from Sub-Saharan Africa with the same qualifications compete for a managerial position in a US-American multinational company? Might it not be that learned historical categories such as 'modern West' and 'inferior non-West', and critical diversity markers such as 'race', 'gender', 'ableism', and so on, inform discourse and practice?

At the same time, we also cannot conclude that such power discrepancies are absolute, for management itself is already a privileged position when compared to the whole of international business. After all, it is mainly outside the managerial field, be it locally or globally, wherein the 'truly' excluded individuals are to be found.

Excluded individuals can be identified via the term 'subaltern' (based on Gramsci, 1971; Spivak, 1988). Subalterns, which means 'being of inferior rank', refers to those towards whom the dominance or hegemony of another group is directed but who do not possess a hegemonic position of their own (e.g. Bhabha, 1994: 59). In terms of this book, you can understand them as individuals subjected to dominant discourses, structures and practices who do not have the agency to resist.

Examples of organizational subalterns are low-wage workers (Ehrenreich, 2001), Filipina maids in Hong Kong (Constable, 1997), domestic servants in Apartheid South Africa (Cock, 1989) and Arab workers in Israel (Drori, 2000). These occupations are bound together by their low-skilled and low-wage character which makes it unlikely that these groups might enable themselves. They don't have a 'voice', so they cannot 'speak' to those in power (Spivak, 1988). Based on this understanding, a 'female, non-white manager from Sub-Saharan Africa', while potentially less enabled than the 'first white guy to win a certain Californian Badminton tournament' (see Chapter 4), might have agency. Even as a slightly marginalized part of the global managerial elite, she can make herself be heard. For a 'female, non-white production worker from Sub-Saharan Africa' at the low-cost production site of a multinational company from 'the West', this might not be possible, and still, she might have more agency and voice than a 'non able-bodied non-white female production worker from Sub-Saharan Africa'.

Nonetheless, we need to doubt that we can 'assess' or 'measure' the hierarchies of CCM, for marginalization and exclusion are more than levels of difference adding up. It seems clear that the 'badminton-playing white guy' is advantaged, but we do not know how the 'female, non-white manager from Sub-Saharan Africa' relates to the 'black Jamaican Rastafarian CEO' (Chapter 4). This insight reminds us that any choice of one group over the other as made by corporate diversity policies might be discriminatory in the end.

When investigating frameworks of power, you will constantly find double or triple marginalizations which are much more consequential than a single ascribed 'non' in an already advantaged managerial identity, and which might point to specific critical intersections. Still, even though others might be even more marginalized, we should not underestimate the biases that exist within the managerial sphere, particularly regarding their impact on individual life experiences and opportunities. I am not saying that the archetypical 'female, non-white manager from Sub-Saharan Africa' is not marginalized – I think she is – I am just questioning whether she should be categorically labelled as powerless, because she might not be a subaltern of international business. Furthermore, we should also consider that CCM might have a responsibility towards those outside the managerial sphere. For example, if intercultural trainers provide Western managers with the knowledge and skills to function better when building up a low-cost, non-Western offshore production site, are the trainers not also responsible for the potentially subaltern workers at this site (see also Szkudlarek, 2009; Romani and Szkudlarek, 2014)?

So, can we become *post*colonial in CCM?

Whereas neo-colonialism and neo-imperialism describes historically-rooted power-discrepancies between 'colonizers' and 'colonized' (in the wider sense), *post*colonialism discusses how to overcome and move beyond these dominant dichotomies (Jack and Westwood,

2009: 11–17). It also stresses cultural flows and processes of translation and appropriation. Read from a postcolonial viewpoint, the life of M.K. Gandhi, for example, is a story both of discriminatory colonial and imperial power *and* of an unforeseen enabling process of resistance and subversion which brought about system change. Likewise, the Jamaican Rastafarian CEO is not only marginalized – he also turns his experiences into a successful photo exhibition. The young cosmopolitan female German co-worker in a traditional male-dominate provincial German company who becomes entangled in a fight over the meaning of a 'handshake' (see Chapter 4) might not only be marginalized by some, but also be advantaged over the local workforce in terms of her employability on the international job market. Still, postcolonialism also acknowledges that something like 'subalternity' exists, and that not everyone meets in 'third spaces' and negotiates meaning.

Therefore, again, we need to juggle and combine multiple perspectives in context. Pierre Bourdieu's (1983, 1986) notion of symbolic capital (see Chapter 1)might help us to determine who still has 'enough' resources to compete and enable themselves, and who is excluded and disabled due to a lack of (symbolic) capital.

Alternatively, Gavin Jack and Robert Westwood (2009: 11-15) have suggested four aspects to a postcolonial CCM (I have broadened these from colonizer–colonized relations to asymmetrical power relations in general). We are first asked to investigate the context-specific motivation, experiences, effects, and so on, of interactions in asymmetrical power relations. We are, secondly, required to become and remain aware that dominance and hegemony as processes are resisted, appropriated and counteracted by those being subjected to it. We should also acknowledge that while colonization might have come to an end, the legacies of colonial relations still bring about neo-colonial facets of managerial theory and practice, and related systems of knowledge and power. Finally, these considerations should give back 'voice' to those who are marginalized and silenced by dominant discourses (subalterns).

While I support the first three points, I am not quite sure whether it is possible to give subalterns a voice: for if I speak for 'them', how can I be sure that I get it right and do not misrepresent others? For example, we might re-examine my attempts at 'giving voice' to a 'Muslim woman wearing a headscarf' or a 'black Rastafarian Jamaican CEO': maybe I have just stereotyped them even further by singling them out, albeit with the best postcolonial and critical intentions. In the end (as deconstruction informs us), every counter-argument confirms the dominant argument. Still, at least another voice might be heard. Hence, any counter-practice might still be the better practice (in the sense of a more equal, fair and authentic CCM), even though it is just the intermediate step towards the actual goal – namely moving beyond dominant configurations of power/knowledge.

For instance, in managerial literature there is a widespread yet theoretically unjustified (Guo and Al Ariss, 2015) practice to refer to a moving individual from the 'non-West' as an implicitly unskilled 'migrant', and to a moving individual from 'the West' as an implicitly skilled 'expatriate' (Al Ariss and Crowley-Henry, 2013). As a power-sensitive and historically-aware CCM student or practitioner, you will notice that these categories are informed by neo-colonial categories of centre and periphery, 'West' and 'non-West', and 'Global North and South'. You are then asked to investigate your own corporate practice. It might be that your company – located in a Western European country of your choice – currently internationalizes and seeks highly-qualified employees from elsewhere. As could happen, the best applicants might be individuals from Muslim countries with an international career path.

You might now start to reflect upon processes of identification and recognition (see Chapter 4) and become aware that the label chosen changes according to how a person is perceived. 'Ethnic minority' stresses 'race', 'migrant' stresses 'movement of inferior status', 'expatriate' stresses 'movement of superior status', and 'Muslim' presumes that 'religiousness' trumps other identifications. So which label are you going to choose in this context?

As history informs us, there is a high risk that these (from their own emic perspective) 'highly-skilled expatriates' will be perceived as 'inferior migrants' who are constructed as 'non-Western' and 'traditional' (based on an Orientalist discourse). You might also expect that 'Western' society will treat them as negatively 'different', and maybe you will need to ask yourself whether your company should do something about that.

To prevent misperceptions, you would need to look back at societal categories of identity, recognition and belonging, and question yourself and corporate practice – otherwise, you might not succeed in moving beyond the dominant discourse. If you have identified a certain societal practice as neo-colonial or neo-imperialist, it might be better not to mirror it on a corporate level. For instance, you should not underestimate your new co-workers' ability to learn the language of your country, as is often done in obligatory integration or immigration classes.

Finally, you would need to try to establish rules of practice that make sure your new Muslim co-workers are not alienated on the grounds of simple signs such as 'not shaking hands with a woman' (if they are male) or 'wearing a headscarf' (if they are female). You might also think of involving your new co-workers in these corporate processes of sense-making and refrain from prescribing what should be done *for* them, as you know that this restricts agency and risks losing sight of alternative perspectives. (Instead of speaking *for* them, let them have a voice of their own.) Finally, you should ask yourself what can I (and we, as individuals and as an organization) learn from this new and unexpected internationality in our midst? Who else needs to be considered, and which perspective is lost? How can we create new, power-sensitive and historically-aware *inter*cultural meanings, practices, structures etc. together?[5]

Biases in CCM and intercultural training

From a power-sensitive perspective, CCM and intercultural training contexts cannot be power-free. Even though we might be unsure of the specifics (Is it discourses, structures, practices or agency? How do history, knowledge and power intersect?); power *must* be part of a particular context somehow. We might well assume that discourse, structure, practice and agency keep each other in balance *in general* (culture mostly works out). However, *in particular*, it might happen that this balance is lost, and that dominant discourses, structures and practices rob certain individuals of their agency. Often, these power-discrepancies are rooted in history, and colonialism and imperialism, which brought about the dominant knowledge of 'how to view the world', are a major factor to consider.

A power-sensitive practice requires us to identify those critical intersections which disadvantage certain individuals. Critical intersections are based on general frameworks of power, but only manifest themselves in particular, that is in specific contexts, within specific boundary conditions, and concerning specific individuals (or all of these together). For those who are totally 'without voice', the term subaltern has been suggested; still, we need to assume that there are many more, less absolute and particular power effects.

These considerations remind us that there is no universal guideline about 'how to become postcolonial' in CCM – for particular power effects unravel from individual experience – but only guiding questions regarding how we might investigate CCM practice in context. So what are the prominent biases of CCM and intercultural training, and how might they influence us and others in specific situations and under specific circumstances? To speak in terms of conceptualizations of intercultural competence (see Chapter 3), raising these questions will enable us to see and experience more in a more complex manner *in particular contexts*, and this will change and improve CCM *in general*. To this end, I would like to propose some aspects of CCM to which we should pay particular and power-sensitive attention.

The comparative cross-cultural perspective assumes culture to be universal, yet the cultural orientations developed from this perspective have mainly originated in 'the West' and for a specific purpose. The very concept that cultural dimensions are based on – 'national cultures' – can be considered ethnocentric, for it is only in Western Europe and some other parts of the world that national structures overlap with socio-cultural and linguistic identifications.

Cultural dimensions are bipolar opposites, and 'Western' countries often represent the desirable pole, such as performance orientation, individualism or low power distance (Primecz, Romani and Topçu, 2015). Implicit to this is a developmentalist and ethnocentrist world-view. For instance, some scholars have argued that it is only in 'complex societies' that individualism develops to the maximum (Triandis, 1995) or that collective orientations are a remnant of communism which needs to be overcome (Trompenaars and Hampden-Turner, 1997). This implies that all societies develop or should develop in one direction, and that it is the 'Western' world which is more advanced (Chen and Starosta, 2005: 27). Such a viewpoint results in a biased view of culture (Fougère and Moulettes, 2011) and a tendency to portray 'non-Western' countries as more traditional or limited by culture (e.g. Tipton, 2008; Mahadevan, Müller and Pauer, 2012; Moore, 2015b).

The dialectical thinking underpinning cultural dimensions (that is, thinking in contrasting terms such as high versus low power distance) has specific European roots (Rehbein, 2010). In other regions of the world, for example in India, seemingly contrasting categories, such as good and evil, are not necessarily opposite. In Hinduism, one believes in rebirth and death is nothing to be feared. The godly principle can approach humans in many forms (incarnations), and most godly incarnations are known in different versions (male and female, good and evil), all of whom one can pray to. In Chinese philosophy, the principle of Yin and Yang implies that seemingly opposite (e.g. male and female) forces are interrelated and complementing each other. We can therefore critique a theory of culture which is based on opposing categories as ethnocentrist. We might even ask, what would CCM theory and practice look like if one of these alternative worldviews had become dominant?[6]

The cultural perspective wishes to critique mainstream comparative CCM by stressing the need to learn and experience culture in context. However, anthropology itself can be linked back to the period of colonialism during which Western scholars – frequently members of the colonial administration or missionaries – studied traditional and non-Western communities from a superior point of view (D. Lewis, 1973). It is debated whether current anthropology has actually succeeded in freeing itself from this past (de l'Estoile, 2008). For instance, how can we be sure that the ethnographer does not impose her/his view of culture onto those studied (Clifford, 1983; Clifford and Marcus, 1986)? Might the ethnographer not also hold etic viewpoints which create artificial Otherness (Fabian, 1983)? Additionally, the very concept of culture and how it is used (Kuper, 1999) is linked to power. Who, for instance, has the 'better' or 'more developed' culture? Whose cultural values should become the global norm, and why do some people believe in their cultural supremacy?

The intercultural approach proposes alternative tools for interculturally competent interactions, for instance, emic(s) and etic(s). However, such an approach presupposes a negotiation of meaning on 'equal terms'; it tends to overlook critical diversity categories and the power effects of how individuals identify and recognize others as similar or different (see Chapter 4). Focusing solely on the micro-level of interpersonal interactions might also neglect the wider frameworks of power, for instance, corporate, societal or global hierarchies, wherein these encounters take place (Halualani and Nakayama, 2010). Simply speaking, the perspective of those in power tends to prevail, regardless of whether it's etic or emic.

Many models of intercultural competence also tend to have a strong focus on language proficiency, based on the conceptualization of culture as communication by E.T. Hall. Still, research on biculturality suggests that language proficiency does not equal cultural competence, and that one might exist without the other (Brannen and Thomas, 2010). From a critical perspective, language might even be part of the problem. The competencies of individuals who are not fluent in the dominant language – often English, but sometimes another one – might be underestimated (Vaara, Tienari, Peikkari and Säntti, 2005). In multicultural teams, asymmetrical *lingua franca* fluency might create mutually exclusive identities of 'us' versus 'them' (Hinds, Neeley and Cramton, 2013).

Intercultural training intends to deliver *useful* advice for specific contexts, the implicit assumption being that a trained individual will 'function better'. But who is actually being trained and for what purposes? Historically, the needs of the US-American Foreign Service Institute were linked to hegemonic geo-politics after World War II (Leeds-Hurwitz, 1990). This reminds us that concepts such as intercultural competence have been developed to explicitly dominate or at least implicitly manipulate others. In international business, it is mainly 'Western' managers who receive intercultural training (Szkudlarek, 2009), because it is they who are the strategically important resource to be invested in. Often the standard tool for doing so is a mono-directional preparatory training, focusing on national cultural differences. Such practice affirms the intercultural trainers' expertise (Dahlén, 1997; Mahadevan, 2011a) and can easily be rationalized and evaluated by corporate HR (Mahadevan, Müller and Pauer, 2012).

As a result of these critical configurations, intercultural training activities as a whole tend to present the world 'through Western eyes' (Szkudlarek, 2009), and – in the terminology of subaltern studies – the 'non-Western others' who are the object of these training activities cannot 'speak back'. This might result in the creation of an over-trained Western managerial elite equipped with the know-how for dominating less valuable corporate resources and the vast majority of non-Western 'others' who remain undertrained (Szkudlarek, 2009). So how can we make sure that neglected 'others' are fairly represented and have equal opportunities in CCM as well?

In the end, all intercultural training and educational activities ask us to change to 'who we are' and 'how we (should) behave'. However, as Betina Szkudlarek (2009) has pointed out, this might result in a lack of honesty, authenticity and sincerity when communicating and interacting. This insight questions the whole intercultural training and education business, for *why* should a trained individual be more 'interculturally competent' than any other individual with good observation skills, high levels of empathy and the ability to learn from others who has not been 'trained'? We should therefore question the presumed need to perform as the only goal against which intercultural competence is measured. We should also remind ourselves of the need to be authentic as social human beings who need to relate to other social beings in a way that is honest and sincere.

Intercultural training activities are also not commissioned by companies out of social altruism. They need to contribute to corporate success, and they need to do so in a cost-efficient and cost-effective manner, and this means that the 'need to train' has to be sold. So what about the ethics of intercultural trainers (Romani and Szkudlarek, 2014) and the power mechanisms of the intercultural training triangle (Mahadevan and Mayer, 2012)? The market value of intercultural trainers is boosted if they present themselves as the experts to 'overcome difference' (Dahlén, 1997), and for this market value to manifest itself, national cultural differences and their negative effects have to be presented as sufficiently detrimental to corporate success (Dahlén, 1997; Mahadevan, 2011a).

Such a practice might further affirm national cultural differences – which might already be presupposed by the participants, for example, as based on learned imaginative geographical categories. These learned differences can then be used by people to defend their own interests in a multinational cooperation in times of crisis: for instance, engineers based in Western headquarters who fear being laid off might find proof of non-Western offshoring engineers' inferior capabilities in cultural dimensions (Mahadevan, 2011a). This reminds us that all knowledge is a tool of power, and that intercultural knowledge, too, might be used for identity-related mechanisms of defence.

These insights challenge the very assumption that culture is tacit and pre-reflexive and that individuals in cross-cultural encounters might not be aware of cultural explanations. Rather, it might well be that individuals *use* culture strategically and to their best interests, and this is a power issue. For instance, when 'Russianness' is expected by corporate superiors in a company internationalizing to Russia, an otherwise bicultural and internationally mobile individual might 'play the Russian' in order to secure themselves a job (Mahadevan and Zeh, 2015). Likewise, bicultural (often bilingual) individuals, who are often viewed as a cultural asset to organizations (Brannen and Thomas, 2010), may use their boundary-spanning abilities to exclude others. Therefore, culture itself is power as well.

Moving beyond the biases of CCM and intercultural training requires a power-sensitive and historically-aware practice. For in doing so we are asked to understand power in terms of discourse, structure, practice and agency, to question our own knowledge of the world and its historic roots, and to consider the requirements of a postcolonial CCM. We might reach these goals by investigating the intersections of power/knowledge and history from multiple angles (as exemplified by the previous discussion of 'what history means for CCM'). To make the task small and manageable, this concluding section has directed the spotlight towards those facets of CCM and intercultural training that seem to require a power-sensitive and historically-aware practice the most.

Power effects can only be unravelled from particular contexts. This requires us to translate between macro and micro, and between comparative and ethnographic tools (Chapter 2), to investigate both cultural regularity and variability as negotiated meanings in ritualized intercultural interactions (Chapter 3), and to consider the interrelations between power, identification and recognition from multiple viewpoints (Chapter 4). Still, in the end, power is a personal thing, and our individual responsibilities might differ based on 'who we are', the contexts to which we have access, and the power effects we create, affirm, experience, resist or simply do not notice (Chapter 5). So are you part of the discursive 'West' or from the 'non-West', or do you identify as a 'halfie' beyond this dichotomy, and how should this matter to you and others in CCM?

Notes

1   Michel Foucault (with Gordon, 1980) suggests that 'knowledge is power and power is knowledge'. He therefore speaks of 'power/knowledge' as a singular concept of two semi-directional, interrelated and complementary processes.
2   Southeast Asia, that is the countries south of China (if not part of Greater China, such as Singapore) and east of India, tends to be neglected in comparative CCM theory. For instance, there are no GLOBE study cultural dimensions for this region. To my mind, the reason for this might be the astonishing internal heterogeneity and the history of constant change that characterize Southeast Asia (D.G.E. Hall, 1981). Therefore, comparative cross-cultural concepts which are based on the assumption of an internally homogeneous national culture might not fit (the other reason could be that India and Greater China are more economically-relevant or even increasingly 'dangerous' competitors in the eyes of the West, as was Japan in the 1980s).
3   The concepts of centre and periphery, as put forward by World Systems Theory (e.g. Wallerstein, 1974), are central to analysing the legacies of imperialism and colonialism. World Systems Theory emerged in the 1970s, mainly originating from sociology, and has developed into a highly interdisciplinary field. One of its major thinkers was Immanuel Wallerstein, who traced the development of modern capitalism back to its roots in the 15th to 17th centuries, thereby highlighting the socially, culturally and historically contingent nature of today's business knowledge (Wallerstein, 1974). Generally speaking, World Systems Theory critiques the state as the major unit of analysis, aims at overcoming disciplinary schisms (e.g. within the social sciences and between the social sciences and history) and wishes to transcend the structures of knowledge inherited from the 19th century. For CCM, its ideas raise the important question as to whether presumably rational, culture-free and modern managerial theory, knowledge and practice might not actually be contingent upon the social, cultural and historical context wherein it emerged and perpetuate historical imbalances of power. The dichotomy between centre and periphery is an example of such a contingency.
4   In peninsular Southeast Asian colonies, mainly Malaysia, Indians were employed as unskilled plantation workers and not as administrative middlemen (see D.G.E. Hall, 1981).
5   For the underlying real-life case behind these suggestions, please read Mahadevan (2012c) and Mahadevan and Kilian-Yasin (2016).

6   Tony Fang (2012) has proposed a Yin and Yang theory of culture wherein he argues that you can approach culture as encompassing all orientations simultaneously, like Yin-Yang philosophy suggests. However, at least to my mind, this is a counter-theory to dominant discourse which does not enable us to move *beyond* dominant dichotomies. It still works within the confinements of the national cultural container, it is still based on dualities, and it does not overcome the 'West' versus 'non-West' divide. As an anti-theory to 'Western' cultural dimensions, it might become the new 'how to do it' if successful.

Concluding remarks

This book sketched the contours of a critical CCM. All chapters involved facets of interplay, aiming at an anthropologically-inspired, culturally-aware and power-sensitive reflexive practice. The concluding remarks summarize what has been done, what is required for a critical CCM, and why this should matter.

What has been done?

Chapter 1 introduced a culturally-aware, anthropologically-informed approach to CCM (which moves beyond how culture is normally understood in a CCM text). It examined culture as 'that shared, learned and social complex whole' which permeates every aspect of human life. The awareness of wider facets of culture, such as meaning, knowledge, behaviour, being-in-the-world, and objects and technology, and the skills with which to investigate them in context, were considered 'cultural essentials for CCM'. Still, not every aspect of culture as 'that complex whole' is equally relevant to a specific CCM situation, and therefore we are required to juggle different assumptions of what culture might involve when experiencing it. This is the first facet of interplay as proposed by this book. Such cultural awareness in particular contexts enables us to consider neglected facets of culture: those aspects which are not part of the traditions of cross-cultural management and intercultural communication. The first is a largely positivist field with often language-based research methods; the second investigates interpersonal interactions with the help of linguistic models and views culture as communication, which only includes selected aspects of 'the whole of culture'. Both favour selected aspects of culture over others. For instance, the *Routledge Companion to Cross-Cultural Management* (edited by Nigel Holden, Snejina Michailova and Suanne Tietze, 2015) dedicates one out of five sections to 'language and languages', including critical perspectives, yet does not cover embodiment, that is how we perceive others and the world through the body. Still, if considered, embodiment has implications for CCM: research suggests that female managers need to adapt to male expectations on the female body (e.g. Tretheway, 1999). The issue seems aggravated for female managers who are labelled 'non-Western', for they need to meet two dominant expectations, namely a cultural ('Western') and a gender-related (male) expectation (e.g. Gonaraghi and Dye, 2016). If both are incommensurable, they might result in a 'no-win scenario', and a single embodied sign of 'otherness' – such as an Indian female manager wearing a sari – might rob an individual of her agency (Mahadevan, 2015a). This suggests that we need to consider the whole of culture and not only selected aspects of it when we investigate its consequences for CCM.

Comparative CCM investigates relative national cultural differences with the help of bipolar cultural dimensions (Chapter 2). It favours large-scale language-based and positivist research over the small-scale ethnographic comparison of several micro-cultures. This macro-universalist approach might neglect alternative facets of culture; in specific micro-contexts, it needs to be balanced by an ethnographic frame of mind. Such an act of interplay between macro-universalist and micro-relativist tools makes the cross-cultural manager a detective who cares about cultural puzzles.

Despite culture being a group phenomenon, it is individuals who interact with each other. The intercultural perspective, put forward in Chapter 3, is based on the assumption that macro-cultural differences will manifest themselves in the micro-cultural interactions between members of different cultures. Conceptualizations of intercultural competence and cultural intelligence focus on the processes and components of successful CCM on the interrelated levels of skills, knowledge, behaviour, motivation and interest. The differentiation between emic and etic was considered as a major tool for overcoming difference. Again, complementary viewpoints might enrich this perspective. For instance, as anthropological ritual theory suggests, the intercultural interactionist approach might be best suited to ritualized interactions (e.g. negotiations) but less applicable to complex interactions (e.g. multicultural teamwork). The paradoxical finding that intercultural interactions are both regular and variable might be balanced by a focus on negotiated symbolic meanings in ritualized interactions, and this constitutes a further act of interplay, as proposed by this book.

Chapter 4, entitled 'Diversity and Identity', introduces additional considerations which are not yet considered by CCM but allow for more authentic and equal acts of identification. Culture was understood as processes of identification and recognition on multiple levels by which individuals give *meaning* to perceived differences and its presumed origins. Viewing culture in terms of collective identities seemed fruitful for understanding subjective culture as related to meaning, knowledge, behaviour, being-in-the-world and interpretation, but might not deliver full insights into the objective cultural frameworks wherein individuals act. We should therefore substitute culture with collective identity, while keeping in mind that national and societal structures and institutions *do* contribute to cross-national differences. If we confuse the two concepts, we create artificial national cultural containers, overestimate macro-level cross-cultural difference, and exaggerate the permanence of 'national cultures'. An overview on the intercultural triangle highlighted that the perceptions of difference are often linked to the motivations and interests held by a specific group of people to perceive others as negatively different in order to affirm themselves of their own collective identity. In this process, some groups might be historically, systematically or structurally disadvantaged, and these are the critical power implications of workplace diversity. This suggests that intercultural interactions are not power-free and that conceptualizations of intercultural competence fail to account for this factor. Generally speaking, human beings seem prone to exaggerating some differences and minimizing others. 'Large' markers of difference, originating from societal, national or dominant discursive classifications, might be taken as proof for individuals actually *being different* in a specific context, whereas 'small' differences might go unnoticed. Likewise, 'small' differences, which might not have mattered at all, may become insurmountable and the object of plays of power when being interpreted as 'large-scale' and 'fundamental'. We also need to bear in mind that individuals tend to attach judgements to the perception of difference, and it is usually the norms of our own identification(s) which are the highly valued ones. We are therefore required to consider critical diversity markers such as race, gender, ethnicity or religion for CCM. For a more authentic practice, we need to 'read between the lines' of the identity categories that seem 'true' to us. Such a deconstruction of the mechanisms of identification, recognition, marginalization and exclusion constitutes the next sphere of interplay.

Chapter 5 put forward a power-sensitive perspective to CCM which acknowledges the impact of power, history and knowledge. It investigated multiple interrelated facets of power, such as discourse (how a concept informs our real-life experiences and vice versa), structure (the institutions, economic policies, laws, etc. which are informed by discourse and made manifest via our actions), agency (how individuals have the power to resist, subvert or change structure and discourse via their actions), and practice (how individuals act within these structures, and as related to discourse and agency). Several examples, such as the imagined categorizations of the world into 'West' and 'non-West', suggested that power is intertwined with our presumably 'objective' knowledge of the world. Furthermore, specific historic events, such as colonialism and imperialism, have informed the present interrelations between power/knowledge in CCM. These effects were made visible through a discussion of the implicit biases of cross-cultural management and intercultural training. On the other hand, individuals also translate and appropriate meaning and power in unforeseen ways and enable themselves. All these effects merge in particular contexts. This reminds us that we can only investigate CCM practice from the experience itself and need to trace phenomena across multiple contexts. The ability to understand the power effects in CCM from specific situations, understood as nodes of power, and as related to all 'frameworks of power', is another major facet of interplay suggested by this book.

The overarching idea of this book was to bring together multiple CCM perspectives in order to facilitate their critical interplay in practice. This approach was based on the assumption that CCM is a multi-disciplinary field and that, instead of engaging in a fruitless debate of 'which perspective is better than the other', we should rather ask ourselves how we might utilize the benefits of this diversity. This ability is a key aspect of intercultural competence, and if we direct this goal towards the knowledge foundations of our discipline, this might be the first step towards a multi-paradigmatic interplay in practice.

This book also tried to put forward the notion that CCM unravels from its contexts. These contexts are *particular*, which means that we might approach them with a *general* critical awareness, but that we need to experience culture in context in order to find out which perspective matters, which tool to choose, and how to combine perspectives and tools for a anthropologically-inspired and power-sensitive practice. From my experience, CCM contexts are becoming increasingly complex and glocal; they offer more choices and combinations, yet simultaneously require more complex decisions to be made. They tend to involve an increasing amount of technology, and they have moved beyond the merely managerial sphere towards questions of joint operations management, shared virtual servers, collaborative engineering, and so on. Across many contexts, the 'cross-cultural' has seeped into the social and the professional, and it might be impossible to separate it out again. Hence, a critical awareness of cultural essentials (Chapter 1) and the ability to gain wider insights from cultural particularities in specific contexts seem indispensable social competences, also for our everyday lives.

Following this understanding, this book was not about a general 'critical anti-theory' in the sense of Marx (1985 [1844]), the employment of which will bring about a pre-defined 'ideal world'. To me, this would imply that being 'critical' becomes the new 'how to do it', and this is not my understanding of how to be critical. Rather, I have tried to envisage a constructive and positive process of *adding* to our understanding of CCM and the social world which evolves from experiencing culture in context. This might involve multiple techniques, such as anthropologically-inspired cultural-awareness, reflexivity, deconstruction or a general power sensitivity, which have been proposed in this book. Likewise, postcolonial, to me, is more than 'anti-colonial' – rather, it involves an attempt to move *beyond* the dominant discourse, structures and practices, for example, by tracing cultural flows and translation beyond simple colonizer–colonized dichotomies.

What is required and why should it matter?

To my mind, the ability to move back and forth between perspectives and identify unexpected relations in presumed contradictions (a reflexive interplay) lies at the heart of a critical CCM.

When envisaging such a practice, I am not thinking in terms of 'ethics', as, for instance, Betina Szkudlarek (2009), Laurence Romani and Betina Szkudlarek (2014) and Terence Jackson (2011) have done. Not because I am against ethics; the word just seems too big to me. I am also not certain that we can establish ethics for CCM which, in the end, is about how worldviews are not universal and about how culture manifests itself in multiple, context-specific ways. In line with this thought, I suggest unravelling the requirements for 'being ethical' from particular contexts as well, be they empirical investigations (if CCM is to be studied or researched upon) or managerial practice (if CCM needs to be 'done').

Despite being potentially valuable in theory, holding multiple paradigms in mind is difficult in practice (Romani, Primecz and Topçu, 2011): we could keep paradigms in mind simultaneously, we could employ them one after the other (the sequential approach), or we could constantly move back and forth across them via interplay (Schultz and Hatch, 1996).

Which strategy to employ in practice depends on the context and purposes to be achieved. For instance, if you are charged with suggesting new international markets for a specific corporate product or service, then in-depth, interpretative investigations might not be feasible in a business world driven by return on investment, efficiency and effectiveness. At this point, comparing relative national markets via available quantitative comparisons might be a good first choice. However, after having employed this tool and narrowed down your choices, you might then proceed to qualitative interviews to investigate the context in detail: a sequential approach.

Or, if you are a corporate representative from country X charged with selecting a joint venture partner from country Y, you might as well start with comparing national cultural differences between country

X and Y. If these match, this can be a first assumption of joint venture compatibility. However, you should also ask yourself whether your corporate culture actually fits with the general quantitative descriptions of country X that you have encountered. If this is not the case, and if country Y has already been determined as the country of origin of your future joint venture partner, then you should proceed qualitatively and try to find a partner who is as 'culturally untypical' for country Y as your company seems to be for country X. Again, this would mean employing a sequential approach, although on multiple levels.

On the other hand, if you wish to uncover culture in context, for example during first-contact business negotiations (a classic intercultural training scenario), this might be best done via the interplay between potentially complementary perspectives, for instance cultural dimensions and ethnographic frame of mind, cultural variability and regularity, ritualized versus complex interactions, and so on.

Interplay requires moving back and forth across perspectives. Firstly, you should investigate what these perspectives have in common; secondly, you should analyse how they are different; finally, you should ask yourself how these different viewpoints can enrich your understanding of a specific context. For instance, in a first-contact business negotiation, you could investigate whether you might identify cultural dimensions in the interaction. Having done this, you might ask yourself what you can learn when approaching the interaction from an ethnographic frame of mind. By viewing both perspectives in light of each other, you may be able to identify how *exactly* pre-existent macro-cultural differences and emergent micro-level processes of meaning-making, both of which are part of the interaction, come together. If you can then reflect upon the fruitfulness of the interplay, you might find additional angles from which to proceed, and the next interpretative cycle begins.

Interplay seems the most feasible multi-perspective approach to CCM practice (unless a sequential approach is self-evident), for it allows you to switch between paradigms, yet only requires holding a single perspective in mind *at a time*. For example, at one time you could ask questions about culture, at another time you might balance the limitations of this approach by observing tacit culture and embodied behaviour, and when you combine both aspects, you might uncover the gap between what people say they do and what they actually do (e.g. Mahadevan, 2013). Conversely, the simultaneous approach to multiple paradigms might be the most difficult to achieve (Romani, Primecz and Topçu, 2011), for it requires the highest awareness *at a time*.

The previous considerations are the reason why I chose interplay as the guiding principle to structure this book. My understanding of a *critical* interplay is that it requires reflexivity, anthropologically-inspired cultural awareness and a grounded sensitivity towards questions of power. To facilitate such cultural awareness (which goes beyond how the term is defined in intercultural competence research), this book embarked from a cultural perspective (Chapter 1) and acknowledged multiple cultures and identities (Chapter 4). For a higher sensitivity regarding power, it included critical diversity considerations and multiple identifications (Chapter 4), and a postcolonial discussion of frameworks of power (Chapter 5).

This means that this book complemented established cross-cultural and intercultural approaches with a 'cultural perspective', a 'critical multiple cultures perspective' and a 'power-sensitive perspective', all three of which are my own wording. The cultural, the cross-cultural and the intercultural perspective were considered to be the foundations of the CCM triangle (Chapters 1–3). Constructing a three-dimensional pyramid upon it, the critical multiple cultures and the power-sensitive perspective (Chapters 4–5) brought this triangle to the next level. This approach was based on the assumption that it is only the combination of all five perspectives that does justice to the whole of our CCM experiences.

Interplay *with others* is required regarding our individual attempts at 'being critical', which only emerges in relation with others (Adorno, 1975). For example, as Hans-Georg Gadamer (1960) has argued, humans might not be able to develop 'free' knowledge beyond the confinements of their own history and society. This suggests that even our attempts at 'moving beyond' are culturally-relative and can never constitute a universal 'critical truth': they are a relational practice in context.

We are therefore asked not only to 'take CCM apart', but also to 'add and build something' from this experience. Mats Alvesson and Kaj Sköldberg's (2000) differentiation between D-reflexivity and R-reflexivity might be helpful for doing so. D-reflexivity refers to practices of deconstruction, R-reflexivity to the constructive processes thereafter which build new structures, processes, frames, etc. To me, CCM is an exercise in both; with the cautious note of never to feel too sure about being on the right track (for instance, if cultural knowledge is used strategically by many diverging interest groups, how can you be sure that *you* are the one to change the context for the better?).

Our identities being relational, we need to deconstruct and reconstruct CCM *together* in order to move beyond the biases of our respective selves. This means that reflexivity, too, emerges in interaction with and is partly steered by others (Hibbert, Coupland and MacIntosh, 2010; Mahadevan, 2011b, 2012b), and needs to be directed towards the whole of culture (Mahadevan, 2015a). Such a relational approach enables us to acknowledge more facets of culture and the social embeddedness of managerial practice (Parker, 2002; Grey, 2013: 8). It reminds us that we, as single individuals, can neither become 'fully aware', nor are we individually able to define 'how things should work'.

My underlying views on management and organizations were based on a stakeholder rather than a shareholder perspective (Cairns and Śliwa, 2008, based on Freeman, 1984). This perspective assumes that organizations (and managers acting within this sphere) are not and should not be merely profit-oriented but need to consider stakeholders, that is those within and beyond the organizational sphere who have an interest in the organization and related managerial actions (such as workers, consumers, societies, governments, non-governmental organizations, societies, local communities, ecology, etc.).

A stakeholder perspective on CCM asks us to actively pursue the question of how CCM *should* be configured to meet social human needs which go beyond mere profit-oriented and economic requirements. Asking this question might be more important than having all the answers. It reminds us that we are never 'finished' in the sense that we just 'do' CCM and cannot discover anything anymore when re-examining ourselves and others, a concept or tool, or a situation.

To steer this process, we might consider prudent questions such as (adapted from Flyvbjerg, 2001: 60) where are we going? Is this development desirable? What, if anything, should be done about it (and who should do it)? Who gains and who loses, and by which mechanisms of power? In the end, however, CCM might just be about 'experiencing more and more complex things' in context, and to draw conclusions from there, as conceptualizations of intercultural competence suggest.

For example, the problem with dominant discourse is that it creates mutually exclusive identities and oversimplifies reality in the interests of some over others. Yet whereas power in general is a big concept, investigating power in context is not usually an earth-moving thing. It might mean noticing the newspaper headline on the 'first non-Asian guy' to win a certain badminton tournament in the San Francisco Bay Area, or asking yourself if there is something wrong with international management if a black Jamaican Rastafarian CEO frequently experiences body-searches for no particular reason and wondering how this might make *you* feel. It is a personal motivation and interest to care about things, and the decision is yours and mine alone. I personally, for instance, wanted to find out what it felt like to be categorized as Muslim in Munich directly after the attacks on the New York World Trade Center on September 11, 2001, so I wore a headscarf in town. My perception was that it changed how others viewed me, that I was treated as more different, and that I felt much less at home. What I have learned from this experience is that it is the simple things that create big, power-laden realities, so we need to start small, in our own prac- tice, and try to walk in the other's shoes a little bit. We could learn something about how the world looks from another perspective, and, if we are lucky, we might contribute to a more equal and fair CCM.

Ultimately, there might be no grand theory of how to be critical in CCM. The best we can do (together) might be to question ourselves and our implicit assumptions, to pay attention to particular power relations, to test power-sensitive hypotheses in context, to juggle different per- spectives and tools, and to do so regarding all facets of power, all CCM stakeholders and all aspects of culture (or at least as many facets, stake- holders and aspects as we can become aware of and juggle in practice). Still, whether such a practice does more good than harm (and who will judge this and how?) remains to be seen.

The wider challenge obviously lies in integrating this practice within a framework that is part of the problem, namely management and international business, the corporate environments wherein we act, and the problematic worldviews and histories which inform them. The only thing we might be able to do about this is to decide that we *want* to concern ourselves with an anthropologically-inspired, culturally-aware and power-sensitive reflexive practice which is more than a merely instrumental CCM. Its purposes and outcomes do not lie in your and my hands alone, but it is still 'us' who *are* the system.

Potentially, our joint critical practice might bring about a reflexive, culturally-aware and power-sensitive CCM *and* enrich our lives in the process. It remains to be seen whether we can actually make the world a better place (and who has to be enabled or needs to enable themselves for doing so), but what harm can it do to live trying to move beyond a few constraints of our own?

References

Abu-Lughod, L. (1991) 'Writing against culture', in R. Fox (ed.), *Recapturing Anthropology: Working in the Present*. Santa Fe: School of American Research Press. pp. 117–135.

Acker, J. (2012) 'Gendered organizations and intersectionality: problems and possibilities', *Equality, Diversity and Inclusion: An International Journal*, 31(3): 214–224.

Adorno, T.W. (1975) *Negative Dialektik [Negative Dialectics]*. Frankfurt am Main: Suhrkamp.

Al Ariss, A. and Crowley-Henry, M. (2013) 'Self-initiated expatriation and migration in the management literature', *Career Development International*, 18(1): 78–96.

Alvesson, M. and Deetz, S. (2000) *Doing Critical Management Research*. London: Sage.

Alvesson, M. and Deetz, S. (2006) 'Critical theory and postmodernism approaches to organizational studies', in S. Clegg, C. Hardy, T. Lawrence and W. Nord (eds), *The Sage Handbook of Organization Studies*. London/Thousand Oaks, CA/New Delhi: Sage. pp. 255–283.

Alvesson, M. and Sköldberg, K. (2000) *Reflexive Methodology: New Vistas for Qualitative Research*. London: Sage.

Appadurai, A. (1995) 'Playing with modernity: the decolonization of Indian cricket', in C. Breckenridge (ed.), *Consuming Modernity: Public Culture in a South Asian World*. Minneapolis, MN: University of Minnesota Press. pp. 23–48.

Aristotle (2004/1955 [350 BC]) *The Ethics of Aristotle: The Nicomachean Ethics*. Penguin Classics. Edited by J.A.K. Thomson. Re-issued 1976, revised by Hugh Tredennick. Harmondsworth: Penguin.

Ashkanasy, N., Gupta, V., Mayfield, M. and Trevor-Roberts, E. (2004) 'Future orientation', in R. House, P. Hanges, M. Javidan and V. Gupta (eds), *Culture, Leadership, and Organizations: The GLOBE Study of 62 Societies*. Thousand Oaks, CA/London/New Delhi: Sage. pp. 282–342.

Bachmann-Medick, D. (2009) *Cultural Turns*. Reinbek bei Hamburg: Rowohlt.

Ballmer, S. (2001) 'I love this company', www.youtube.com/watch?v=f__n8084YAE [last accessed 1 July 2016].

Banerjee, B. and Prasad, A. (2008) 'Guest editorial: Introduction to the Special Issue on critical reflections on management and organizations: a postcolonial perspective', *Critical Perspectives on International Business*, 4(2/3): 90–98.

Barmeyer, C. (2004) 'Learning styles and their impact on cross-cultural training: an international comparison in France, Germany and Quebec', *International Journal of Intercultural Relations*, 28(6): 577–594.

Barnard, A. (2000) *History and Theory in Anthropology*. Cambridge: Cambridge University Press.

Barner-Rasmussen, W. (2015) 'What do bicultural-bilinguals do in multinational corporations?', in N. Holden, S. Michailova and S. Tietze (eds), *The Routledge Companion to Cross-Cultural Management*. London: Routledge. pp. 142–150.

Baumann, G. (1996) *Contesting Culture: Discourses of Identity in Multi-ethnic London*. Cambridge: Cambridge University Press.

Bendl, R., Eberherr, H. and Mensi-Klarbach, H. (2012) 'Vertiefende Betrachtung zu ausgewählten Diversitätsdimensionen' [In-depth view on selected dimensions of diversity], in: R. Bendl, E. Hanappi-Egger and R. Hofmann (eds), *Diversität und Diversitymanagement* [Diversity and Diversity Management]. Wien: UTB-Facultas. pp. 79–135.

Bennett, J.M. and M.J. Bennett (2004) 'Developing intercultural sensitivity: an integrative approach to global and domestic diversity', in D. Landis, J.M. Bennett and M.J. Bennett (eds), *Handbook of Intercultural Training*. Thousand Oaks, CA/London/New Delhi: Sage. pp. 147–165.

Bennett, M.J. (1986) 'A developmental model approach to training for intercultural sensitivity', *International Journal of Intercultural Relations*, 10(2): 179–186.

Berger, P. and Luckmann, T. (1966) *The Social Construction of Reality*. New York: Doubleday.

Berger, P. and Luckmann, T. (1995) *Modernity, Pluralism and the Crisis of Meaning*. Gütersloh: Bertelsmann Foundation.

Bhabha, H.K. (ed.) (1990) *Nation and Narration*. London: Routledge.

Bhabha, H.K. (1994) *The Location of Culture*. London: Routledge.

Bjørge, A.K. and Whittaker, S. (2015) 'Corporate values: a linguistic approach', *International Journal of Cross-Cultural Management*, 15(3): 347–362.

Boas, F. (1896) 'The limitations of the comparative method of anthropology', *Science*, 4(103): 901–908.

Boje, D.M. (2008) *Storytelling Organizations*. London and New York: Sage.

Bourdieu, P. (1977) *Outline of a Theory of Practice*. Cambridge: Cambridge University Press.

Bourdieu, P. (1983) 'Ökonomisches Kapital, kulturelles Kapital, soziales Kapital' ['Economic capital, cultural capital, social capital'], in R. Kreckel (ed.), *Soziale Welt* [*Social World*], Special Issue on *Soziale*

Ungerechtigkeiten [*Social Injustices*]. Translated by R. Kreckel. Göttingen: Otto Schartz. pp. 183–198.

Bourdieu, P. (1986) 'The forms of capital', in J. Richardson (ed.), *Handbook of Theory and Research for the Sociology of Education*. New York: Greenwood Press. pp. 241–258.

Boussebaa, M. and Morgan, G. (2014) 'Pushing the frontiers of critical international business studies: the multinational as a neo-imperial space', *Critical Perspectives on International Business*, 10(1/2): 96–106.

Brannen, M.Y. (2004) 'When "Mickey" loses face: recontextualization, semantic fit and the semiotics of foreignness', *Academy of Management Review*, 29(4): 593–616.

Brannen, M.Y. and Thomas, D.C. (2010) 'Bicultural individuals in organizations: implications and opportunity', *International Journal of Cross-Cultural Management*, 10(1): 5–16.

Buckley, P.J. and Chapman, M. (1997) 'The use of native categories in management research', *British Journal of Management*, 8(4): 283–300.

Bührmann, A. (2015) 'Gender: a central dimension of diversity', in S. Vertovec (ed.), *Routledge International Handbook of Diversity Studies*. London and New York: Taylor and Francis. pp. 23–42.

Byram, M. (1997) *Teaching and Assessing Intercultural Communicative Competence*. Clevedon: Multilingual Matters.

Cairns, G. and Śliwa, M. (2008) *A Very Short, Reasonably Cheap and Fairly Interesting Book about International Business*. London: Sage.

Callon, M. (1986) 'Some elements of a sociology of translation: domestication of the scallops and the fishermen of St Brieuc Bay', in J. Law (ed.), *Power, Action and Belief: A New Sociology of Knowledge? Sociological Review Monograph 32*. London: Routledge. pp. 196–223.

Carr, A. (2006) 'In the constructive tradition of being critical', *Critical Perspectives on International Business*, 2(2): 73–78.

Carter, C., Clegg, S. and Kornberger, M. (2008) *A Very Short, Reasonably Cheap and Fairly Interesting Book about Strategy*. London: Sage.

Chen, G.-M. and Starosta, W.J. (2005) *Foundations of Intercultural Communication*. Lanham, MD: University of America Press.

Chevrier, S. (2009) 'Is national culture still relevant to Management in a global context? The case of Switzerland', *International Journal of Cross-Cultural Management*, 9(2): 169–183.

Chhokar, J.S., Brodbeck, F.C. and House, R.J. (eds) (2007) *Culture and Leadership across the World: The GLOBE Book of In-Depth Studies of 25 Societies*. Mahwah, NJ: Erlbaum.

Clark, B.R. (1972) 'The organizational saga in higher education', *Administrative Science Quarterly*, 11(2): 178–184.

Clegg, S. (1989) *Frameworks of Power*. London/Thousand Oaks, CA/New Delhi: Sage.

Clifford, J. (1983) 'On ethnographic authority', *Representations*, 1(2): 118–146.

Clifford, J. and Marcus, G.E. (eds) (1986) *Writing Culture: The Poetics and Politics of Ethnography*. Berkeley, CA and London: University of California Press.

Cock, J. (1989) *Maids and Madams: Domestic Work under Apartheid*. London: The Women's Press.

Comte, A. (1907) *A General View of Positivism*. London: Routledge.

Constable, N. (1997) *Maid to Order in Hong Kong: Stories of Filipina Workers*. Ithaca, NY and London: Cornell University Press.

Cooke, B. (2004) 'The managing of the (third) world', *Organization*, 11(5): 603–629.

Critchley, S. (1992) *The Ethics of Deconstruction: Derrida and Levinas*. Edinburgh: Edinburgh University Press.

Csordas, T.J. (1990) 'Embodiment as a paradigm for anthropology', *Ethos*, 18(1): 5–47.

Czarniawska, B. (1998) *A Narrative Approach to Organization Studies*. London: Sage.

Dahlén, T. (1997) *Among the Interculturalists: An Emergent Profession and its Packaging of Knowledge*. Stockholm: Gotab.

D'Andrade, R. (1995) *The Development of Cognitive Anthropology*. Cambridge: Cambridge University Press.

Deal, T.E. and Kennedy, A.A. (1982) *Corporate Culture: The Rites and Rituals of Corporate Life*. Boston, MA: Addison-Wesley.

Deardorff, D.K. (2006) 'Identification and assessment of intercultural competence as a student outcome of internationalization', *Journal of Studies in International Education*, 10(3): 241–266.

Deardorff, D.K. (ed.) (2009) *The Sage Handbook of Intercultural Competence*. Thousand Oaks, CA/London/New Delhi/Singapore: Sage.

Deetz, S. (1992) 'Critical interpretive research in organizational communication', *Western Journal of Speech Communication*, 46: 131–149.

de l'Estoile, B. (2008) 'The past as it lives now: an anthropology of colonial legacies', *Social Anthropology*, 16(3): 267–279.

Derrida, J. (1978) *Writing and Difference*. Translated by A. Bass. London and New York: Routledge.

Dilley, S. (ed.) (1999) *The Problem of Context*. Oxford and New York: Berghahn.

d'Iribarne, P. (2009) 'National cultures and organisations in search of a theory: an interpretative approach', *International Journal of Cross-Cultural Management*, 9(3): 309–321.

d'Iribarne, P. (2012) *Managing Corporate Values in Diverse National Cultures: The Challenge of Difference*. London: Routledge.

Drori, I. (2000) *The Seam Line: Arab Workers and Jewish Managers in the Israeli Textile Industry*. Stanford, CA: Stanford University Press.

Durham, D. (1999) 'The predicament of dress: polyvalency and the ironies of cultural identity', *American Ethnologist*, 26(2): 389–411.

Earley, P.C. and Ang, S. (2003) *Cultural Intelligence: Individual Interactions across Cultures*. Palo Alto, CA: Stanford University Press.

Ehrenreich, B. (2001) *Nickel and Dimed: Undercover in Low-Wage USA*. London: Granta.

Emrich, C.G., Denmark, F.L. and Den Hartog, D.N. (2004) 'Cross-cultural differences in gender egalitarianism: implications for societies, organizations and leaders', in R. House, P. Hanges, M. Javidan and V. Gupta (eds), *Culture, Leadership, and Organizations: The GLOBE Study of 62 Societies*. Thousand Oaks, CA/London/New Delhi: Sage. pp. 343–394.

Eriksen, T.H. (2010) *Small Places, Large Issues*. London: Pluto Press (1st edn, 1995).

Eriksen, T.H. and Nielsen, F.S. (2013) *A History of Anthropology*. London: Pluto Press (1st edn, 2001).

Essers, C. and Benschop, Y. (2009) 'Muslim businesswomen doing boundary work: the negotiation of Islam, gender and ethnicity within entrepreneurial contexts', *Human Relations*, 62(3): 403–423.

Fabian, J. (1983) *Time and the Other: How Anthropology Makes its Object*. New York and Chichester: Columbia University Press.

Fang, T. (2012) 'Yin and yang: a new perspective on culture', *Management and Organization Review*, Special Issue on *Indigenous Management Research in China*, 8(1): 25–50.

Flyvbjerg, B. (2001) *Making Social Science Matter: Why Social Inquiry Fails and How it can Succeed Again*. Cambridge: Cambridge University Press.

Forstenlechner, I. and Al-Waqfi, M.A. (2010) 'A job interview for Mo, but none for Mohammed', *Personnel Review*, 39(6): 767–784.

Foucault, M. and Gordon, C. (1980) *Power/Knowledge: Selected Interviews and Other Writings 1972–1977*. New York: Pantheon Books.

Fougère, M. and Moulettes, A. (2011) 'Disclaimers, dichotomies and disappearances in international business textbooks: a postcolonial deconstruction', *Management Learning*, 43(1): 5–24.

Fox, K. (2004) *Watching the English: The Hidden Rules of English Behaviour*. London: Hodder & Stoughton.

Freeman, R.E. (1984) *Strategic Management: A Stakeholder Approach*. Boston, MA: Pitman.

Frenkel, M. (2008) 'The MNC as a third space: rethinking IM knowledge through Homi Bhabha', *Academy of Management Review*, 33(4): 924–942.

Frenkel, M. and Shenhav, Y.A. (2006) 'From binarism back to hybridity: a postcolonial reading of management and organization studies', *Organization Studies*, 24(6): 855–876.

Furnivall, J.S. (1956) *Colonial Policy and Practice*. Cambridge: Cambridge University Press (1st edn, 1948).

Gadamer, H.-G. (1960) *Wahrheit und Methode* [*Truth and Method*]. Tübingen: Mohr.

Gallagher, J. and Robinson, R. (1953) 'The imperialism of free trade', *The Economic History Review*, 6(1): 1–15.

Gannon, M.J. and Pillai, R. (2010) *Understanding Global Cultures: Metaphorical Journeys through 29 Nations, Clusters of Nations, Continents and Diversity*. Los Angeles and London: Sage (1st edn, 2009).

Garsten, C. (1994) *Apple World: Core and Periphery in a Transnational Organizational Culture*. Stockholm: Gotab.

Geertz, C. (1973) *The Interpretation of Cultures: Selected Essays*. New York: Basic Books.

Gertsen, M.C., Søderberg, A.-M. and Zølner, M. (2012a) 'Introduction and overview', in M.C. Gertsen, A.-M. Søderberg and M. Zølner (eds), *Global Collaboration: Intercultural Experiences and Learning*. New York: Palgrave Macmillan. pp. 1–15.

Gertsen, M.C., Søderberg, A.-M. and Zølner, M. (2012b) 'Final perspectives', in M.C. Gertsen, A.-M. Søderberg and M. Zølner (eds), *Global Collaboration: Intercultural Experiences and Learning*. New York: Palgrave Macmillan. pp. 255–268.

Gesteland, R.R. (2012) *Cross-Cultural Business Behaviour: A Guide for Global Management* (5th edn). Copenhagen: Copenhagen Business School Press (1st edn, 2009).

Gilmartin, M. (2009) 'Colonialism/Imperialism', in C. Gallagher, C.T. Dahlman, M. Gilmartin, A. Mountz and P. Shirlow (eds), *Key Concepts in Political Geography*. Thousand Oaks, CA: Sage. pp. 115–123.

Goffman, E. (1959) *The Presentation of Self in Everyday Life*. New York: Doubleday.

Goffman, E. (1963) *Stigma: Notes on the Management of Spoiled Identity*. London: Simon & Schuster.

Goffman, E. (1974) *Frame Analysis: An Essay on the Organization of Experience*. London: Harper & Row.

Golnaraghi, G. and Dye, K. (2016) 'Discourses of contradiction: a postcolonial analysis of Muslim women and the veil', *International Journal of Cross-Cultural Management*, 16(2): 137–152.

Golnaraghi, G. and Mills, A.J. (2017) 'Diversity discourses and corporate Canada: unveiling images of the Muslim woman at work', in J. Mahadevan and C.-H. Mayer (eds), *Muslim Minorities, Workplace Diversity and Reflexive HRM*. London: Taylor and Francis.

Goxe, F. and Paris, M. (2016) 'Traveling through the class ceiling? Social mobility of "traditional" and "new" expatriates', *International Journal of Cross-Cultural Management*, 16(2): 171–189.

Gramsci, A. (1971) *Selection from Prison Notebooks*. New York: International Publishers.

Grey, C. (2013) *A Very Short, Reasonably Cheap and Fairly Interesting Book about Studying Organizations*. London: Sage (1st edn, 2005).

Gudykunst, W.B., Wiseman, R.L. and Hammer, M.R. (1977) 'Determinants of a sojourner's attitudinal satisfaction: a path model', in B. Ruben (ed.), *Communication Yearbook 1*.Brunswick, NJ: Transaction. pp. 415–425.

Gullahorn, J.R. and Gullahorn, J.E. (1962) 'An extension of the U-curve hypothesis', *Journal of Social Issues*, 3: 33–47.

Guo, C. and Al Ariss, A. (2015) 'Human resource management of international migrants: current theories and future research', *International Journal of Human Resource Management*, 26(10): 1287–1297.

Hall, B.J. (2005) *Among Cultures: The Challenge of Communication*. Fort Worth, TX: Harcourt College.

Hall, D.G.E. (1981) *A History of South East Asia* (4th edn). London: Palgrave Macmillan (1st edn, 1959).

Hall, E.T. (1959) *The Silent Language*. Garden City, NY: Doubleday.

Hall, E.T. (1966) *The Hidden Dimension*. Garden City, NY: Doubleday.

Hall, E.T. (1976) *Beyond Culture*. Garden City, NY: Doubleday.

Hall, E.T. (1983) *The Dance of Life: The Other Dimension of Time*. Garden City, NY: Doubleday.

Hall, S. (1990) 'Cultural identity and diaspora', in J. Rutherford (ed.), *Identity, Community, Culture, Difference*. London: Lawrence and Wishart. pp. 222–237.

Halualani, R.T. and Nakayama, T.K. (2010) 'Critical intercultural communication studies: at a crossroads', in T.K. Nakayama and R.T. Halualani (eds), *The Handbook of Intercultural Communication*. Chichester: Wiley-Blackwell. pp. 1–15.

Hannerz, U. (1990) 'Cosmopolitans and locals in world culture', *Theory, Culture and Society*, 7(2): 237–251.

Hannerz, U. (2004) 'Cosmopolitanism', in D. Nugent and J. Vincent (eds), *Companion to the Anthropology of Politics*. Oxford: Blackwells.

Hatch, M.J., with Cunliffe, A. (2006) *Organization Theory: Modern, Symbolic and Postmodern Perspectives*. Oxford: Oxford University Press (1st edn, 1996).

Hibbert, P., Coupland, C. and MacIntosh, R. (2010) 'Reflexivity: recursion and relationality in organizational research processes', *Qualitative Research in Organizations and Management*, 5(1): 47–62.

Hicks, D. and Beaudry, M.C. (2010) *The Oxford Handbook of Material Culture Studies*. Oxford: Oxford University Press.

Hinds, P.J., Neeley, T.B. and Cramton, C.D. (2013) 'Language as a lightning rod: power contests, emotion regulation, and subgroup dynamics in global teams', *Journal of International Business Studies*, 45(5): 536–561.

Ho, K. (2009) *Liquidated: An Ethnography of Wall Street*. Durham, NC and London: Duke University Press.

Hobsbawn, E.J. (1989) *The Age of Empire, 1875–1914*. London: Abacus Books.

Hobson, J.A. (1902) *Imperialism: A Study*. Cambridge, MA: Harvard University Press.

Hofstede, G. (1980) *Culture's Consequences: International Differences in Work Related Values*. Beverly Hills, CA: Sage.

Hofstede, G. (2001) *Culture's Consequences: Comparing Values, Behaviors, Institutions and Organizations across Nations*. London/Thousand Oaks, CA/New Dehli: Sage.

Hofstede, G. (2006) 'What did GLOBE really measure? Researchers' minds versus respondents' minds', *Journal of International Business Studies*, 37(6): 882–896.

Hofstede, G. (2010) *Cultures and Organizations: Software for the Mind*. New York: McGraw-Hill.

Hofstede, G. and Bond, M. (1988) 'The Confucius connection: from cultural roots to economic growth', *Organizational Dynamics*, 16(4): 4–21.

Holden, N. (2002) *Cross-Cultural Management: A Knowledge Management Perspective*. Harlow: Pearson Education/Prentice Hall.

Holden, N., Michailova, S. and Tietze, S. (2015) *The Routledge Companion to Cross-Cultural Management*. London: Routledge.

Holgersson, C., Tienari, J., Meriläinen, S. and Bendl, R. (2016) 'Executive search as ethnosociality: a cross-cultural comparison', *International Journal of Cross-Cultural Management*, 16(2): 153–169.

Honold, P. (2000) 'Culture and context: an empirical study for the development of a framework for the elicitation of cultural influence in product usage', *International Journal of Human-Computer Interaction*, 12(3–4): 327–345.

House, R., Hanges, P., Javidan, M. and Gupta, V. (eds) (2004) *Culture, Leadership, and Organizations: The GLOBE Study of 62 Societies*. Thousand Oaks, CA/London/New Delhi: Sage.

House, R. and Javidan, M. (2004) 'Overview of GLOBE', in R. House, P. Hanges, M. Javidan and V. Gupta (eds), *Culture, Leadership, and Organizations: The GLOBE Study of 62 Societies*. Thousand Oaks, CA/London/New Delhi: Sage. pp. 9–28.

Howe, S. (2002) *Empire: A Very Short Introduction*. Oxford: Oxford University Press.

Jack, G. and Westwood, R. (2009) *International and Cross-Cultural Management Studies: A Postcolonial Reading*. Basingstoke: Palgrave Macmillan.

Jackson II, R.L. and Hogg, M.A. (2010) *Encyclopedia of Identity* (Vol. 1). Thousand Oaks, CA/New York/New Delhi/Singapore: Sage.

Jackson, T. (2011) *International Management Ethics: A Critical, Cross-Cultural Perspective*. Cambridge: Cambridge University Press.

Jackson, T. (2013) 'Reconstructing the indigenous in African management research: implications for international management studies in a globalized world', *Management International Review*, 53(1): 13–38.

Jackson, T. (2014) 'Editorial: Cross-cultural management from the South: what a difference global dynamics make', *International Journal of Cross-Cultural Management*, 14(1): 3–5.

Javidan, M., House, R. and Dorfman, W. (2004) 'A nontechnical summary of GLOBE findings', in R. House, P. Hanges, M. Javidan and V. Gupta (eds), *Culture, Leadership, and Organizations: The GLOBE Study of 62 Societies*. Thousand Oaks, CA/London/New Delhi: Sage. pp. 29–48.

Jones, M.O. (1996) *Studying Organizational Symbolism: What, How, Why?* Thousand Oaks, CA/London/New Delhi: Sage.

Kedia, B.L. and Mukherji, A. (1999) 'Global managers: developing a mindset for global competitiveness', *Journal of World Business*, 24(3): 230–215.

Kipling, R. (1899) 'The white man's burden', *McClure's Magazine*, 12 February.

Klarsfeld, A. (ed.) (2010) *International Handbook on Diversity Management at Work*. Cheltenham: Edward Elgar.

Kluckhohn, C. and Strodtbeck, K. (1961) *Variations of Value Orientations*. Westport, CT: Greenwood Press.

Konrad, A.M., Prasad, P. and Pringle, J.K. (eds) (2006) *Handbook of Workplace Diversity*. Thousand Oaks, CA and London: Sage.

Kroeber, A.L. and Kluckhohn, C. (1952) 'Culture: a critical review of concepts and definitions', *Papers of the Peabody Museum of American Archeology and Ethnology*, 47(1). Cambridge, MA: Peabody Museum.

Kuper, A. (1999) *Culture: The Anthropologists' Account*. Cambridge, MA and London: Harvard University Press.

Landis, D., Bennett, J.M. and M.J. Bennett, M.J. (eds) (2004) *Handbook of Intercultural Training*. Thousand Oaks, CA/London/ New Delhi: Sage.

Latour, B. (1996) 'On actor-network theory: a few clarifications', *Soziale Welt [Social World]*, 47(4): 369–381.

Lawler, S. (2008) *Identity: Sociological Perspectives*. Cambridge and Malden, MA: Polity Press.

Leeds-Hurwitz, W. (1990) 'Notes in the history of intercultural communication: the Foreign Service Institute and the mandate for intercultural training', *Quarterly Journal of Speech*, 76(3): 262–281.

Levay, C. (2014) 'Obesity in organizational context', *Human Relations*, 67(5): 565–585.

Lewis, D. (1973) 'Anthropology and colonialism', *Current Anthropology*, 14(5): 581–602.

Lewis, R.D. (1996) *When Cultures Collide: Leading across Cultures*. London: Nicholas Brealey International.

Lewis, R.D. (2012) *When Teams Collide: Managing the International Team Successfully*. London: Nicholas Brealey International.

Mahadevan, J. (2010) 'Personalvorteil Bi-Kulturalität: Chance für Bikulturelle' [Human resource advantage bi-culturality: an opportunity for bicultural individuals], *Personal [Personnel]*, December: 26–28.

Mahadevan, J. (2011a) 'Engineering culture(s) across sites: implications for cross-cultural management of emic meanings', in H. Primecz, L. Romani and S. Sackmann (eds), *Cross-Cultural Management in Practice: Culture and Negotiated Meaning*. London: Elgar. pp. 156–174.

Mahadevan, J. (2011b) 'Reflexive guidelines for writing organizational culture', *Qualitative Research in Organizations and Management*, 6(2): 150–170.

Mahadevan, J. (2012a) 'Are engineers religious? An interpretative approach to cross-cultural conflict and collective identities', *International Journal of Cross-Cultural Management*, 12(1): 133–149.

Mahadevan, J. (2012b) 'Translating nodes of power through reflexive ethnographic writing', *Journal of Organizational Ethnography*, 1(1): 119–131.

Mahadevan, J. (2012c) 'Utilizing identity-based resistance for diversity change: a narrative approach', *Journal of Organizational Change Management*, 25(6): 819–834.

Mahadevan, J. (2013) 'Performing interplay through intercultural simulations: insights on tacit culture in Taiwanese–German management team', *International Journal of Cross-Cultural Management*, 13(3): 243–263.

Mahadevan, J. (2015a) 'Caste, purity, and female dress in IT India: embodied norm violation as reflexive ethnographic practice', *Culture and Organization*, 21(5): 366–385.

Mahadevan, J. (2015b) 'Understanding the process of intercultural nego-tiations through liminality: insights on bi-culturality, marginality and cultural expertise from a Sino-German business context', *International Journal of Cross-Cultural Management*, 15(3): 239–258.

Mahadevan, J. and Kilian-Yasin, K. (2016) 'Dominant discourse, Orientalism and the need for reflexive HRM: skilled Muslim migrants in the German context', *International Journal of Human Resource Management*, pp. 1–23. doi:10.1080/09585192.2016.1166786.

Mahadevan, J. and Mayer, C.-H. (2012) 'Guest Editorial: Collaborative approaches to intercultural engineering', *Intercultural Engineering*, Special Issue of *Interculture Journal*, 18: 5–15.

Mahadevan, J., Müller, F. and Pauer, V. (2012) 'Interkulturelle Trainings: Chance oder Risiko?' ['Intercultural training: opportunity or risk?'] *Personalwirtschaft* [*Personnel Administration*], March: 57–59.

Mahadevan, J. and Zeh, J.S. (2015) 'Third-country graduates and their transition to the German labor market', *Equality, Diversity and Inclusion: An International Journal*, 34(4): 325–345.

Majumdar, R.C., Raychaudhuri, H.C. and Datta, K. (1978) *An Advanced History of India* (4th edn). Madras (Chennai): Macmillan India (1st edn, 1946).

Malinowski, B. (1922) *Argonauts of the Western Pacific: An Account of Native Enterprise and Adventure in the Archipelagoes of Melanesian New Guinea*. London: Routledge and Kegan Paul.

Marcus, G.E. (1995) *Ethnography through Thick and Thin*. Princeton, NJ: Princeton University Press.

Marx, K. (1985) 'Ökonomisch-philosophische Manuskripte' ['Economical-philosophical manuscripts'], in *Marx-Engels-Werke* [Marx-Engels-Works] (Vol. 40). Berlin: Dietz, pp. 465–588 (1st edn, 1844).

Matthewman, J. (2011) *The Rise of the Global Nomad: How to Manage the New Professional in Order to Gain Recovery and Maximize Future Growth*. London: Kogan Page.

Mauss, M. (1925) *The Gift: Forms and Functions of Exchange in Archaic Societies*. London: Routledge.

Maznevski, M. (2012) 'State of the art: global teams', in M.C. Gertsen, A.-M. Søderberg and M. Zølner (eds), *Global Collaboration: Intercultural Experiences and Learning*. New York: Palgrave Macmillan. pp. 187–206.

Maznevski, M.L., Gomez, C.B., DiStefano, J.J., Noorderhaven, N.G. and Wu, P.-C. (2002) 'Cultural dimensions at the individual level of analysis: the cultural orientations framework', *International Journal of Cross-Cultural Management*, 2(3): 275–295.

McCurdy, D.W., Spradley, J.P. and Shandy, D.J. (2005) *The Cultural Experience: Ethnography in Complex Society*. Long Grove, IL: Waveland Press.

McSweeney, B. (2009) 'Dynamic diversity: variety and variation within countries', *Organization Studies*, 30(9): 933–957.

Mead, G.H. with Morris, C.W. (eds) (1934) *Mind, Self, and Society*. Chicago, IL: University of Chicago Press.

Mead, M. (1963) 'Papers in honor of Melville J. Herskovits: socialization and enculturation', *Current Anthropology*, 4(2): 184–188.

Merleau-Ponty, M. (1965) *Phenomenology of Perception*. London: Routledge and Kegan Paul (1st edn., 1945).

Mik-Meyer, N. (2016) 'Othering, ableism and disability: a discursive analysis of co-workers' construction of colleagues with visible impairments', *Human Relations*, pp. 1–23. doi: 10.1177/0018726715618454.

Minkov, M. (2007) *What Makes Us Different and Similar: A New Interpretation of the World Values Survey and Other Cross-Cultural Data*. Sofia: Klasika i Stil.

Minkov, M. (2011) *Cultural Differences in a Globalizing World*. Bingley: Emerald.

Minkov, M. and Hofstede, G. (2012) 'Is national culture a meaningful concept? Cultural values delineate homogeneous national clusters of in-country regions', *Cross-Cultural Research*, 46(2): 133–159.

Moore, F. (2015a) 'An unsuitable job for a woman: a "native category" approach to gender, diversity and cross-cultural management', *International Journal of Human Resource Management*, 26(2): 216–230.

Moore, F. (2015b) 'Towards a complex view of culture: cross-cultural management, "native categories", and their impact on concepts of management and organisation', in N. Holden, S. Michailova and S. Tietze (eds), *The Routledge Companion to Cross-Cultural Management*. London: Routledge. pp. 19–27.

Morrissey, J. (2014) 'Imperialism and empire', in J. Morrissey, D. Nally, U. Strohmayer and Y. Whelan (eds), *Key Concepts in Historical Geography*. London: Sage. pp. 17–26.

Näslund, L. and Perner, F. (2011) 'The appropriated language: dominant stories as a source of organizational inertia', *Human Relations*, 65(1): 89–110.

Nonaka, I. and Takeuchi, H. (1995) *The Knowledge Creating Company: How Japanese Companies Create the Dynamics of Innovation*. New York: Oxford University Press.

Oberg, K. (1960) 'Culture shock and the problem of adjustment to new cultural environments', *Practical Anthropology*, 7: 177–182.

Orr, J. (1996) *Talking about Machines: An Ethnography of a Modern Job*. Ithaca, NY: Cornell University Press.

Osland, J. and Bird, A. (2000) 'Beyond sophisticated stereotyping: understanding cultural sensemaking in context', *Academy of Management Executive*, 14(1): 65–79.

Osterhammel, J. (2005) *Colonialism: A Theoretical Overview*. Princeton, NJ: M. Wiener.

Parker, I. (1992) *Discourse Dynamics*. London: Routledge.

Parker, M. (2002) *Against Management*. Cambridge: Polity Press.

Perlmutter, H.V. and Heenan, D.A. (1974) 'How multinational should your top managers be?', *Harvard Business Review*, 52(6): 121–132.

Peterson, M.F. and Pike, K.L. (2002) 'Emics and etics for organizational studies: a lesson in contrasts from linguistic', *International Journal of Cross-Cultural Management*, 2(1): 5–20.

Phillips, N. and Hardy, C. (2002) *Discourse Analysis: Investigating Processes of Social Construction*. London: Sage.

Pike, K.L. (1967) *Language in Relation to a Unified Theory of the Structures of Human Behavior*. The Hague: Mouton (1st edn, 1954).

Plummer, D.L. (2003) 'Overview of the field of diversity management', in D.L. Plummer (ed.), *Handbook of Diversity Management – Beyond Awareness to Competency Based Learning*. Lanham/New York/Oxford: University Press of America.

Polanyi, M. (1967) *The Tacit Dimension*. New York: Anchor Books.

Pollock, D. and Van Reken, R. (1999) *Third Culture Kids: The Experience of Growing up among Worlds*. London: Nicholas Brealey.

Prasad, A. (2006) 'The jewel in the crown: postcolonial theory and workplace diversity', in A.M. Konrad, P. Prasad and J.K. Pringle (eds), *Handbook of Workplace Diversity*. Thousand Oaks, CA and London: Sage. pp. 121–144.

Prasad, P. (2012) 'Unveiling Europe's civilized face: gender relations, new immigrants and the discourse of the veil in the Scandinavian workplace', in A. Prasad (ed.), *Against the Grain: Advances in Postcolonial Organization Studies*. Denmark: Copenhagen Business School Press. pp. 54–72.

Prasad, P., Pringle, J.K. and Konrad, A.M. (2006) 'Examining the contours of workplace diversity', in A.M. Konrad, P. Prasad and J.K. Pringle (eds), *Handbook of Workplace Diversity*. Thousand Oaks, CA and London: Sage. pp. 1–22.

Primecz, H., Mahadevan, J. and Romani, L. (2016) 'Guest Editorial: Why is cross-cultural management blind to power relations? Investigating ethnicity, language, gender and religion in power-laden contexts', *International Journal of Cross-Cultural Management*, 16(2): 127–136.

Primecz, H., Romani, L. and Sackmann, S.A. (2009) 'Cross-cultural management research: contributions from various paradigms', *International Journal of Cross-Cultural Management*, 9(3): 267–274.

Primecz, H., Romani, L. and Topçu, K. (2015) 'A multi-paradigm analysis of cross-cultural encounters', in N. Holden, S. Michailova and S. Tietze (eds), *The Routledge Companion to Cross-Cultural Management*. London: Routledge. pp. 431–439.

Pusch, M.D. (2004) 'Intercultural training in historical perspective', in D. Landis, J.M. Bennett and M.J. Bennett (eds), *Handbook of Intercultural Training*. Thousand Oaks, CA/London/New Delhi: Sage. pp. 13–36.

Rafaeli, A. and Pratt, M.G. (1993) 'Tailored meanings: on the meaning and impact of organizational dress', *Academy of Management Review*, 18(1): 32–55.

Rathje, S. (2007) 'Intercultural Competence: the status and future of a controversial concept', *Language and Intercultural Communication*, 7(4): 254–266.

Rehbein, B. (2010) 'Critical theory after the rise of the Global South', *Transcience Journal*, 1(2): 1–17.

Robertson, R. (1994) 'Globalisation or glocalisation?', *Journal of International Communication*, 1(1): 33–52.

Romani, L., Primecz, H. and Bell, R. (2014) 'There is nothing so practical as four good theories', in B. Gehrke and M.-T. Claes (eds), *Global Leadership Practices: A Cross-Cultural Management Perspective*. London: Palgrave Macmillan. pp. 13–50.

Romani, L., Primecz, H. and Topçu, K. (2011) 'Paradigm interplay for theory development: a methodological example with the Kulturstandard method', *Organizational Research Methods*, 14(3): 432–455.

Romani, L., Sackmann, S.A. and Primecz, H. (2011) 'Culture and negotiated meanings: the value of considering meaning systems and power imbalances for cross-cultural management', in H. Primecz, L. Romani and S. Sackmann (eds), *Cross-Cultural Management in Practice: Culture and Negotiated Meanings*. London: Elgar. pp. 1–17.

Romani, L. and Szkudlarek, B. (2014) 'The struggles of the interculturalists: professional ethical identity and early stages of codes of ethics development', *Journal of Business Ethics*, 119(2): 173–191.

Sackmann, S.A. (1997) 'Introduction', in S.A. Sackmann (ed.), *Cultural Complexity in Organizations: Inherent Contrasts and Contradictions*. Thousand Oaks, CA/London/New Delhi: Sage. pp. 1–13.

Said, E. (1979) *Orientalism*. New York: Vintage Books.

Said, E. (1993) *Culture and Imperialism*. New York: Vintage Books.

Saunders, M., Lewis, P. and Thornhill, A. (2009) *Research Methods for Business Students*. Harlow: Pearson Education (1st edn, 1997).

Schein, E.H. (1985) *Organizational Culture and Leadership*. San Francisco, CA: Jossey-Bass.

Schnegg, M. (2014) 'Anthropology and comparison: methodological challenges and tentative solutions', *Zeitschrift für Ethnologie* [*Journal of Anthropology*], 139: 55–72.

Schroll-Machl, S. (2003) *Doing Business with Germans: Their Perception, Our Perception*. Göttingen: Vandenhoek & Ruprecht.

Schultz, M. and Hatch, M.J. (1996) 'Living with multiple paradigms: the case of paradigm interplay in organization culture studies', *Academy of Management Review*, 21(2): 529–557.

Schwartz, S.H. (1992) 'Universals in the content and structure of values: theoretical advances and empirical tests in 20 countries', *Advances in Experimental Social Psychology*, 25: 1–65.

Schwartz, S.H. (1994) 'Beyond individualism/collectivism: new cultural dimensions of values', in U. Kim, H.C. Triandis, C. Kagitcibasi, S.C. Choi and G. Yoon (eds), *Individualism and Collectivism: Theory, Method, and Applications*. Thousand Oaks, CA: Sage. pp. 85–119.

Schwartz-Shea, P. and Yanow, D. (2012) *Interpretive Research Design: Concepts and Processes*. London and New York: Routledge.

Smith, L.T. (1999) *Decolonizing Methodologies: Research and Indigenous Peoples*. London: Zed Books.

Smith, P. (2006) 'When elephants fight, the grass gets trampled: the GLOBE and Hofstede projects', *Journal of International Business Studies*, 37(6): 915–921.

Spencer-Oatley, H. and Franklin, P. (2009) *Intercultural Interaction: A Multidisciplinary Approach to Intercultural Communication*. Basingstoke: Palgrave Macmillan.

Spitzberg, B.H. (2000) 'A model of intercultural communication competence', in L.A. Samovar and R.E. Porter (eds), *Intercultural Communication: A Reader*. Belmont, CA: Wadsworth. pp. 375–387.

Spitzberg, B.H. and Changnon, G. (2009) 'Conceptualizing intercultural competence', in D.K. Deardorff (ed.), *The Sage Handbook of Intercultural Competence*. Thousand Oaks, CA/London/New Delhi/Singapore: Sage. pp. 2–52.

Spivak, G.C. (1988) 'Can the subaltern speak?', in C. Nelson and L. Grossberg (eds), *Marxism and the Interpretation of Culture*. Urbana, IL: University of Illinois Press. pp. 271–313.

Spradley, J.P. (1980) *Participant Observation*. Belmont, CA: Wadsworth.

Strathern, M., Crick, M.R., Fardon, E.H., Jarvie, I.C., Pinxten, R., Rabinow, P., Tonkin, E., Tyler, S.A. and Marcus, G.E. (1987) 'Out of context: the persuasive fictions of anthropology [and comments and reply]', *Current Anthropology*, 28(3): 251–281.

Sumner, W.G. (1906) *Folkways*. New York: Ginn.

Syed, J. (2008) 'Employment prospects for skilled migrants: a relational perspective', *Human Resource Management Review*, 18(1): 28–45.

Syed, J. and Özbilgin, M. (2009) 'A relational framework for international transfer of diversity management practices', *International Journal of Human Resource Management*, 20(12): 2435–2453.

Szkudlarek, B. (2009) 'Through Western eyes: insights into the corporate training field', *Organization Studies*, 30(9): 975–986.

Tajfel, H. and Turner, J.C. (1986) 'The social identity theory of intergroup behavior', in S. Worchel and W.G. Austin (eds), *Psychology of Intergroup Relations*. Chicago, IL: Nelson-Hall. pp. 7–24.

The Hofstede Centre (2016a) 'United States', www.geert-hofstede.com/united-states.html [last accessed 15 May 2016].

The Hofstede Centre (2016b) 'Culture Compass', www.geert-hofstede.com/cultural-survey.html [last accessed 15 May 2016].

Thomas, A., Kinast, E. -U. and Schroll-Machl, S. (2003a) *Handbuch Interkulturelle Kommunikation und Kooperation* [Handbook Intercultural Communication and Cooperation](Vol. 1). Göttingen: Vandenhoeck & Ruprecht.

Thomas, A., Kinast, E. -U. and Schroll-Machl, S. (2003b) *Handbuch Interkulturelle Kommunikation und Kooperation* [Handbook Intercultural Communication and Cooperation](Vol. 2). Göttingen: Vandenhoeck & Ruprecht.

Tienari, J., Meriläinen, S., Holgersson, C. and Bendl, R. (2013) 'And then there are none: on the exclusion of women in processes of executive search', *Gender in Management: An International Journal*, 28(1): 43–62.

Tipton, F. (2008) 'Thumbs-up is a rude gesture in Australia: the presentation of culture in international business textbooks', *Critical Perspectives on International Business*, 4(1): 7–24.

Tomlinson, J., Muzio, D., Sommerlad, H., Webley, L. and Duff, L. (2013) 'Structure, agency and career strategies of white women and black and minority ethnic individuals in the legal profession', *Human Relations*, 66(2): 245–269.

Tretheway, A. (1999) 'Disciplined bodies: women's embodied identities at work', *Organization Studies*, 20(3): 423–450.

Tretheway A. (2001) 'Reproducing and resisting the master narrative of decline: midlife professional women's experiences of aging', *Management Communication Quarterly*, 15(2): 183–226.

Triandis, H.C. (1994) *Culture and Social Behaviour*. New York: McGraw-Hill.

Triandis, H.C. (1995) *Individualism & Collectivism*. Boulder, CO and Oxford: Westview Press.

Trompenaars, F. (1993) *Riding the Waves of Culture*. Burr Ridge, IL: Irwin.

Trompenaars, F. and Hampden-Turner, C. (1997) *Riding the Waves of Culture: Understanding Cultural Diversity in Global Business*. London: Nicholas Brealey.

Tsoukas, H. (2003) 'Do we really understand tacit knowledge?', in M. Lyles and M. Easterby-Smith (eds), *The Blackwell Handbook of*

Organizational Learning and Knowledge Management. Oxford: Blackwell. pp. 410–427.

Turner, V. (1977) *The Ritual Process.* Ithaca, NY: Cornell University Press (1st edn, 1969).

Tylor, E.B. (1871) *Primitive Culture: Researches into the Development of Mythology.* London: John Murray.

Tylor, E.B. (1889) 'On a method of investigating the development of institutions: applied to laws of marriage and descent', *Journal of the Anthropological Institute of Great Britain and Ireland*, 18: 245–272.

Vaara, E., Tienari, J., Piekkari, R. and Säntti, R. (2005) 'Language and the circuits of power in a merging multinational corporation', *Journal of Management Studies*, 42(3): 595–623.

Van Laer, K. and Janssens, M. (2011) 'Ethnic minority professionals' experiences with subtle discrimination in the workplace', *Human Relations,* 64(9): 1203–1227.

Van Maanen, J., Manning, P.K. and Miller, M.L. (1996) 'Series editors' introduction', in M.O. Jones (ed.), *Studying Organizational Symbolism: What, How, Why?* Thousand Oaks, CA/London/New Delhi: Sage.

Vertovec, S. (ed.) (2015) *Routledge International Handbook of Diversity Studies.* London and New York: Taylor and Francis.

Vertovec, S. and Cohen, R. (eds) (2002) *Conceiving Cosmopolitanism: Theory, Context and Practice.* Oxford and New York: Oxford University Press.

Wallerstein, I. (1974) *The Modern World-System I: Capitalist Agriculture and the Origins of the European World-Economy in the Sixteenth Century.* New York: Academic Press.

Ward, J. and Winstanley, D. (2003) 'The absent presence: negative space within discourse and the construction of minority sexual identity in the workplace', *Human Relations,* 56(10): 1255–1280.

Weedon, C. (2004) *Identity and Culture: Narratives of Difference and Belonging.* Maidenhead and New York: Open University Press.

Westwood, R. and Jack, G. (2008) 'The US commercial–military–political complex and the emergence of international business and management studies', *Critical Perspectives on International Business*, 4(4): 367–388.

Witte, A. (2012) 'Making the case for a postnational cultural analysis of organizations', *Journal of Management Inquiry*, 21(2): 141–159.

Zanoni, P., Janssens, M., Benschop, Y. and Nkomo, S. (2010) 'Guest Editorial: Unpacking diversity, grasping inequality: rethinking difference through critical perspectives', *Organization*, 17(1): 9–29.

Ziai, A. (2016) *Development Discourse and Global History.* London: Routledge.

Index